OSA AND MARTIN

FOR THE LOVE OF ADVENTURE

KELLY ENRIGHT

LYONS PRESS
GUILFORD, CONNECTICUT
AN IMPRINT OF GLOBE PEQUOT PRESS

To buy books in quantity for corporate use
or incentives, call **(800) 962-0973**
or e-mail **premiums@GlobePequot.com**.

Lyons Press is an imprint of Globe Pequot Press.

All photographs are courtesy of the Martin and Osa Johnson Safari Museum, Chanute, Kansas, unless otherwise noted.

Text design: Sheryl P. Kober
Project editor: Julie Marsh
Layout artist: Melissa Evarts

Library of Congress Cataloging-in-Publication Data is available on file.

ISBN 978-0-7627-6360-3

Printed in the United States of America

10 9 8 7 6 5 4 3 2 1

To my husband, may our adventures be as timeless

CONTENTS

Preface vi
Acknowledgments xi
Introduction xiii

CHAPTER 1
Martin's First Adventure 1

CHAPTER 2
Honeymoon with Cannibals 33

CHAPTER 3
Taking Aim at Africa 73

CHAPTER 4
Living in Paradise 134

CHAPTER 5
Safari Skies 179

CHAPTER 6
Osa Alone 198

Bibliography 211
Index 215

PREFACE

I was a graduate student in search of a research topic a number of years ago when a mentor told me of a zebra-striped book she had picked up in a used bookstore. She told me what she knew of the woman who wrote the imaginatively titled *I Married Adventure*, and I was hooked. I searched the library for a copy of the book, knowing that it would not be difficult to find, given its unusual cloth case, among the bland brown and black bindings on the shelves. Indeed, it stood out among its neighboring travel narratives much like the black and white stripes of a real zebra stand crisp against the dustier hues of the African plains.

As I dipped into her life story, this woman, named Osa John-son, immediately captured my imagination. She was not simply a wife accompanying her husband on his explorations, but the heroine and the heart of those adventures. She lived in such a different world that I wondered how I might make sense of her life—how, for example, could she shoot at an elephant on one page of her narrative and cuddle one in her living room several pages later? But as I learned more about Osa and her husband, Martin, I found them to be remarkably relatable. The honesty and candor found in Osa's books endeared her to me. Her occa-sional outbursts (born from an independent and stubborn mind) and Martin's sometimes unsympathetic but very male reaction struck me as very real. They seemed like the best of companions; a couple who nurtured and challenged each other in both their private and public lives.

I was also intrigued by the fact that while their work con-tributed to science, they were not high-minded academics. They were middle-class Americans who did not consider themselves above catering to that audience. They had no pretensions. Even after Osa was named one of the world's best-dressed women, she

On their last African adventure, Osa and Martin seem as adoring of each other as on the day they wed.

continued to hunt and fish in safari clothes instead of confining herself to high-fashion celebrity.

Even though they were not scientists by training, they were caught up in the wave of the conservation movement that was emerging in the early twentieth century by virtue of being in the right place at the right time. During the end of the 1800s, familiar animals dwindled in numbers or completely disappeared. In the United States the extinction of passenger pigeons and near-extinction of American bison brought awareness to the idea that animals needed protection from overhunting and habitat degradation. Yet hunting for sport remained a conservation strategy. Within what we now broadly call the "conservation movement," a sharp divide existed between "conservationists" and "preservationists." The former, led by the gun-toting adventure seeker Teddy Roosevelt, sought to conserve resources without prohibiting their use. Thus, conservationists regulated landscapes to make the most of available resources while maintaining natural places. Roosevelt proclaimed the value of nature, sport, and hunting in creating strong, rugged, individualistic American men. Preservationists, on the other hand, wished to set aside natural places and wildlife populations so that they might remain unspoiled by humans. Expressed most eloquently by the gentle wanderer John Muir, preservationists viewed nature as a refuge and a solemn place of spiritual renewal.

Martin and Osa first went to Africa, it seems, with little awareness of these domestic conservation conversations. To outdoorsmen in the 1920s, Africa meant hunting safaris. The British colonial government regulated the hunting of some of the top trophy animals, and the Johnsons, like most other visitors to British East Africa, obtained proper permits from the authorities in order to participate. Throughout the era, hunting preserves and permits became increasingly more regulated, though then, as now, such regulation was difficult to enforce in vast, wild places.

By the time Martin and Osa visited Africa the second time, the hobby of "hunting with a camera" instead of a gun was rising in popularity. The image of hunting as a masculine undertaking remained, but the idea of searching for wildlife simply to observe it was growing as well. Thus, when Osa and Martin seem a little trigger-happy in their early days in Africa, they are reflecting typical American ideas about the nature of wild adventures. Through further contact with those intimately involved in regulating and studying wildlife—and in observing the reduction of game numbers themselves—Martin and Osa evolved into more astute observers of nature. We must think of them as reflective of their era and read with an eye to their growing sentiments toward nature. In their works, the meaning of adventure changes from hunting and near-death encounters to glimpses of wildlife in situ and an appreciation for moments of serene observation. In part, their lives and this book are a story of an evolving conservation ethic.

While the Johnsons were typical of their contemporaries in their representations of adventures with animals, they were also typical in the images of native peoples they put before audiences. The racial stereotypes embraced for entertainment purposes in their commercial films are, at times, difficult for today's viewer to watch uncritically. If you read Martin and Osa's books, however, you'll find their attitudes toward native people surprising in a different way. Their relationships with the many Africans they employed as porters, cooks, houseboys, trackers, and gun bearers show admiration for individuals and even attempts to impress them and gain their respect on their own cultural terms. What the films reveal is an attempt to cater to audience expectations. The comparison between book and film shows the Johnsons were quite open-minded in their dealings with different types of people they met on their travels.

What many people (myself included) find most compelling about Osa and Martin, apart from their work, is their relationship. Instead of living predictable, workaday lives, they seemed to be always at play. Though they sometimes revealed the hardships and trials of their chosen lives, it is this playfulness that brings them to life. You can tell by the way they looked at each other in their more casual portraits that they were having fun. You can also tell that they adored and admired each other. They had the kind of love that inspired each other to live as fully as possible. Other biographers have tracked their travels and described the behind-the-scenes details of their professional lives, and these works have been invaluable to my research in outlining geographies and explaining discrepancies. These biographies, however, do not flesh out the development of their experiences in and thoughts about the natural world, nor do they impart to the reader the spirit of Osa and Martin's adventures and personalities, or the full picture of their relationship.

This biography follows their increasing awareness toward wildlife and wild places. In writing it, my hope is to convey the true spirit of Osa and Martin, not as static or flawed celebrity personalities, but as two people who explored and interpreted the world around them as that world, in turn, transformed them. Mark Twain famously proclaimed that travel is death to ignorance. Martin and Osa experienced the horizon-broadening effects of travel firsthand and brought those visions back, hoping to share their love of adventure as well as their respect for unfamiliar places, people, and animals.

ACKNOWLEDGMENTS

My own small adventures inspired much of my interest in Osa and Martin, and those who have shared such adventures contributed to this fascination. My brother, Jeffrey Enright, made the one willow tree in our Jersey City backyard into a wilderness and, along with other adventurous friends, transformed Florida campgrounds into worlds ripe for exploration. While the only wild animals we faced were armadillos, these young wanderings instilled in me the sense, if not the fact, of adventure.

My parents, Dennis and Patricia Enright, expanded my sense of the world when I was very young, taking me to see the pyramids at Giza, German castles, and Venetian canals. Through them I learned that travel is not just the monuments but the moments—the chill of the Egyptian desert at night, the crunch of real French bread on Parisian streets, and the glow of a campfire under summer snow in the Sierras.

My husband, Christopher Imeson, has heroically indulged my penchant for exploration—from crumbling roadside attractions to seaside Mayan ruins. Whether hiking mountain peaks or diving coral reefs, we have found each other, like Martin and Osa, willing partners in adventure.

The staff at the Martin and Osa Johnson Safari Museum in Chanute, Kansas, welcomed me more than once to their archives and assisted my research even from a distance. Museum director Conrad Froehlich provided insights into the Johnsons' world—both past and present. Curator Jacqueline Borgeson guided me through the archives, patiently responded to numerous queries, and quickly turned around photographs for publication. Her work has been invaluable to my own.

When I learned of an editor who had already heard of Martin and Osa, I hoped she would share my passion for their lives.

Holly Rubino has supported and guided this project from its start. Her careful editing and thoughtful questions helped crystallize my ideas, and her enthusiasm for Osa and Martin has no doubt helped make this book what it is.

INTRODUCTION

Martin and Osa were true partners who took turns manning the camera.

In 1932, the same year that Amelia Earhart made the first female solo flight over the Atlantic, a female reporter for the *Wichita Sunday Eagle* wrote an article entitled "Do Women Make Good Explorers?" In it, she posed the questions: "Are women too temperamental to be good explorers? Do they have the physical strength to march endlessly through hot deserts, or the courage to face the perils of the African jungle? Can they calmly follow their leader into the unknown recesses of dark Africa and accept stoically the hardships and dangers which can turn strong men into weak-kneed pawns in the hands of the mighty jungle?" No, replied established male explorers, lunching at what we can only assume is

Osa's natural charm contributed to their success on expedition and on the silver screen.

the Explorers Club in New York City (which did not allow female membership until the 1980s). "One woman," said these men, "can cause more trouble on an exploring expedition . . . than a whole horde of wild elephants, a tribe of wild and blood-thirsty savages, or a dozen lions and tigers ready for food." Women, they asserted, desire too many frivolities on expeditions, bringing an excess of luggage filled with "fine clothes and makeup." Although the men acknowledged that a woman might hold her own when faced with a moment of grave danger, she would not, they insisted, have the emotional fortitude to withstand months of "trifling little things" necessary to travel in the world's jungles.

To all this Martin Johnson told the reporter, "You don't know my wife." She had, he continued, "showed the most remarkable courage of any person I have ever seen in the jungle." Osa Johnson, the reporter claimed, was the first woman given a hunting license in Africa and had "faced more wild beasts in their native habitats than any white explorer, with the exception of her husband." Martin, however, did allow that perhaps not all women were fit for exploration, proclaiming Osa's strengths while questioning if many other of the female sex would have done the same.

"Boots and pants and a clean shirt or so . . . and I'm ready," retorted Osa to the claim that women bring too much luggage on an expedition. "Of course, I do like a tooth brush," she admitted, "but I can get along perfectly well without a compact or lipstick." Furthermore, she argued, since she was smaller than her husband, her luggage was actually more compact. On the other hand, Osa did seem, on film at least, concerned with her appearance. She was acutely aware that she was judged for her beauty, fashion, and charm, as well as for her derring-do. In her lifetime she was considered among British East Africa's most beautiful women and voted one of the world's best dressed.

Though Osa dismissed the comments as "silly prejudice," she pointed out that the skeptical New York gentlemen "have in mind a high-heeled, silk-stockinged young flapper"—a wholly different kind of woman than herself. The newspaper article in which this discussion took place defended female courage as not having had a chance to prove itself: "Mrs. Johnson has proved to the world that women do have the bravery of men—but they often don't get a chance to show it, except when a mouse runs across the room."

In her life's travels Osa had many opportunities to prove her courage. Whether face to face with lions or chasing pests from the corners of the bedroom, she stood as the ideal wife for an exploring man. She was also the perfect partner for a man seeking celebrity. Osa was the star of Martin's films, as well as his companion in making them. Her on-screen charm drew in many viewers, while her real-life charisma charmed press and sponsors alike.

In the course of their twenty years of traveling together—from 1917 to 1937—Martin and Osa Johnson made ten commercial films and more than seventy lecture films. Between them they published 120 articles in publications ranging from the journal of the American Museum of Natural History and *Forest and Stream* to the *Saturday Evening Post* and *Cosmopolitan*. They inspired a comic strip and a kids' club. Osa created a line of clothing—and another of stuffed animals. Advertisers posted their faces in magazines hoping to boost sales of tea, soda, beer, batteries, flashlights, cameras, refrigerators, and beauty products.

Martin and Osa saw their lives as a partnership. The survival of their marriage despite perils, disease, work, and celebrity is quite astonishing. Many exploring couples did not last as long. "I wouldn't think of going any place without Osa," said Martin. "By taking my wife along, we can continue the companionship of our married life, even though we are not in the comforts and luxuries of civilization. We are pals and co-workers, and that is more than a lot of married people can say."

Whether in the jungles of Borneo or on the African plains, Osa clung to her role as housekeeper. Even in places Osa knew they wouldn't stay for very long, she "fussed about the house—quite as if [she were] settling down for at least a year—cleaning it, reorganizing it, routing the deadly scorpions out of the corners, teaching the cook some of the dishes which [she knew] were good for Martin, and between times prowling around the garden with [her] .22 and polishing off the somewhat too numerous snakes." Hunting was part of her normal housework. As homemaker, she was also provider. And providing in the wilderness meant hunting, not walking to the butcher's shop. Osa, who named her autobiography *I Married Adventure,* believed that despite wedding such a rootless lifestyle, her marital duties included making a home wherever they went. "I doubt that ever a woman lived who had a stronger instinct for homemaking than I," she confided, "or a man with greater need for a home than Martin."

After a brief revival of their films in the 1950s, the Johnsons were all but forgotten. Osa's books remained on the market through that decade as well but disappeared for nearly three decades before being republished. Osa's stuffed animals and clothing are now difficult to come by. Even the Martin and Osa Johnson Safari Museum and archive that preserves their memory—located well off the main interstate through Kansas in Osa's hometown, Chanute—contains only a small collection of such paraphernalia. The Johnsons' unique blend of Hollywood celebrity and scientific contributions have perhaps made their legacy difficult to pin down. While their raw footage and observations contributed to wildlife studies, and their commercial films circulated in the world of entertainment, they had been marginalized as bit players in the histories of both wildlife study and film. In recent years, the Johnsons' contributions to wildlife documentary filmmaking have been more recognized, but their work does not tell the whole story of Osa and Martin's adventurous lives.

CHAPTER 1

MARTIN'S FIRST ADVENTURE

Like all sailors, we did not love the sea. It was the eternal menace.
— MARTIN JOHNSON

Of the two native Kansans, it was Martin who first set his sights on adventure. He came by his wanderlust honestly. Martin's father, John Alfred Johnson, had immigrated as a child to the United States from Sweden with his family in 1851. He worked as a news-boy in Chicago and New York before moving to the Black Hills to drive a mule team. Given the assignment of transporting buf-falo hides to Gen. George Armstrong Custer's army who were sta-tioned on the plains fighting Native Americans, John then enlisted in the army. In 1880 he married Lucinda Constant, and they set-tled in Rockford, Illinois, where he began work as a foreman at the Rockford Watch Company. Lucinda was the descendent of late-eighteenth-century settlers from Virginia whose family had moved slowly west—first to Ohio, then Illinois, and finally Mis-souri, where she was born. Their son, Martin Elmer Johnson, was born on October 9, 1884. After five years in Rockford, John grew restless once again. When he saw advertisements for the growing Kansas town of Lincoln, pitched as the perfect frontier town, full of health, fresh air, and opportunity, he and Lucinda packed up their infant son and headed west.

Lincoln was a farming community connected to the Union Pacific Railroad that had reached a population of just over two thousand by the time the Johnson family arrived. They found a place to live in town and rented a shop where John set up a jewelry store. Martin began school in a one-room schoolhouse that became increasingly packed with students as Lincoln's population continued to grow. Not inspired by what he considered repetitive and boring lessons, Martin secretly read Frank Merrill dime novels (his parents did not approve of them) but mostly turned to the outdoors for stimulation. He often ran home from school to hop on his horse and ride past the developing farmland and what remained of the native, undeveloped prairie.

One classmate remembered Martin playing with what was possibly his first camera, saying he was a "boy genius with photography." Martin had taken a photo of his friend's girlfriend and put it onto the face of his watch, which his friend found truly impressive. The pair often swam in the Verdigris River and were the victims of bullies throwing their clothes in the water until Martin challenged them to a fight and rounded up enough pals to scare off the aggressors.

Displeased with the stillness of home and school life, Martin grew restless. He frequently skipped school and ran away from home several times, hopping the train out of Lincoln, usually showing up at the homes of Lucinda's family in the Midwest. Martin finished grade school in Independence, Kansas, and at the age of fourteen, he ran away from home once more. This time, however, he made his way to Chicago, where he found a job taking care of valuable horses—each worth $250—headed to Liverpool, England. With his expenses fully paid by his employer, Martin must have felt like a boy on vacation rather than a hired hand. First he rode the train with the horses to Detroit; from there he took a ferry to Niagara Falls. He was impressed by the waterfall so familiar to him from Eastman Kodak pictures. He toured the Kodak factory, then traveled with the horses to the East Coast to prepare for the overseas trip.

When they arrived in Jersey City, New Jersey, where the horses were to be stabled until boarding the ship, one fell sick and delayed Martin's anticipated trip to Manhattan. Other business on the west side of the Hudson River kept him in New Jersey until the next day, when he finally arrived in the heart of New York City. Martin went to the famous landmarks of the day—the Brooklyn Bridge, the Statue of Liberty, Wall Street, Trinity Church, the Flat-iron Building, and Broadway. "Gee but N.Y. is big," he wrote to his parents, telling them of riding ferries, subways, and elevated lines and "so much more my head is in a whirl." New York impressed him more than Chicago. There, he did not have to dodge burning cinders flying in the air. "[E]very thing is so clean and such tall sky-scrapers that the tallest ones in Chicago would look like midgets to the side of them," he mused.

Martin wrote this letter to his parents on stationery he lifted from the Waldorf Astoria Hotel. "What do you think of the bluff I am putting up?" he asked them. "I just walked in the Waldorf-Astoria and don't pay any attention to the millionaires around me." Brash and confident, Martin had only just begun his travels. But he was proud of how far he had come. "[W]ell you were amazed were you," he asked them, "well—you will be further amazed now—be prepared—I ship for Liverpool early Monday morning with the same horses."

Martin crossed the Atlantic Ocean, tramped around England and Paris, and then returned to the United States. In September he was back in Independence working for his father, whose shop had just begun to carry the latest Eastman Kodak cameras. It was not long, however, before Martin found another outlet for exploration. Seeing an open call for a South Seas expedition with famous adventurer and writer Jack London, Martin quickly sent in an application. London telegraphed Martin and asked if he could cook. Eager to impress, Martin replied yes (even though he could not), and in December he arrived at the writer's home in Oakland, California, and began preparation for the expedition.

Still lacking a high school diploma, Martin now turned to London, his new mentor, to receive all the education required of a young adventurer. Never one to sit still for a formal education, London had left the University of California at Berkeley after only one semester. Even London seemed to see the young man, now in his early twenties, was about to embark on a lifetime of explorations. He wrote to Martin's younger sister, Freda: "It is true that I have stolen your brother away from you. But then he wanted to be so stolen, to go on the long voyage, to behold the fire people, and the tree people, and the people of the great swamp, and the great forest. And if he be not eaten by cannibals, I will return him safely to you."

At the time, Jack London was already the country's most popular adventure writer. He had published his classic novels *The Call of the Wild* and *White Fang,* and dozens of magazine articles. Along with his wife, Charmian Kittredge London, he had designed and built a boat on which to sail to the South Seas. They called it the *Snark*, after an imaginary animal in a Lewis Carroll poem. To Martin, the *Snark* was "a mere cork of a boat." What's more, the crew included no experienced navigator, engineer, sailor, or cook (though the latter was Martin's official role). It consisted of the Londons; Paul H. Togichi, a Japanese immigrant and London's personal servant; Charmian's uncle, yachtsman Roscoe Eames; and Stanford University athlete Herbert (Bert) Stolz.

London conceived of the journey as fodder for his writing and imagination. Most practically, he hoped to publish several articles on the lives of the native people of the South Seas. He wanted to take an anthropological angle—though anthropology was still a young discipline at this time. London had read detailed descriptions of native peoples in the adventure books of his favorite writers, Capt. James Cook and Joseph Conrad. It is likely he became intrigued by the discipline on his 1894 visit to the Chicago World's Columbian Exposition, which hosted the first major anthropological installation in the United States. It introduced the public to foreign cultures and highlighted the "advance" or "evolution" of civilization, ranking non-Western peoples as more "primitive." In addition, the fair hosted a colorful display of native peoples going about their daily routines as best they could. Leading anthropologist Franz Boas (who would start up the Anthropology Department at Berkeley just a few years after London dropped out) curated a Northwest Coast village there. The public found such living exhibits entertaining but, by most accounts, were more amused than educated.

According to Martin, London's agenda was not inflected with this sense of superiority or spectacle. "He would treat of their domestic problems," Martin explained, "social structures; problems of living; cost of living as compared with the cost in the United States; education; opportunities for advancement; general tone of peoples; culture; morals; religion; how they amuse themselves; marriage and divorce problems; housekeeping, and a hundred other topics." London wanted to create an authentic record of the lives of South Seas peoples. As always, however, London also had a more romantic goal: He hoped to find adventure. Whatever that adventure might be, he would write it down. "Well," he joked, "if we're boarded by pirates and fight it out until our deck becomes a shambles, I don't think I'll write about it. And if we're wrecked at sea, and are driven by starvation into eating one another, I'll keep it quiet for the sake of our relatives. And if we're killed and eaten by cannibals, of course I shan't let the American public get an inkling of it."

On April 23, 1907, crowds gathered at the docks of San Francisco to see off the famous writer and his unlikely crew. All of London's bohemian buddies were there, including the poet George Sterling, college football coach James Hopper, and the artist Xavier Martinez. The *Snark* broke from the dock and sailed

Martin (back left) stands between Charmian and Jack London on board the *Snark*. (Courtesy of the University of California-Berkeley, Department of Geography Lantern Slide Collection)

through the sunlit San Francisco Bay, beneath the Golden Gate Bridge, and past Seal Rocks. A reporter sailed through the bay with them, and news photographers snapped shots like mad, claiming in their newspapers this was the last anyone would see of the reckless explorer-author. What with the unseaworthy ship and its inexperienced crew, everyone whispered it would be a miracle if they survived.

When they reached the open ocean, Martin began to prepare his first dinner as ship cook. Peeling onions in the kitchen, which was no bigger than a cupboard, his eyes began to tear so badly it was all he could do to get the roast in the oven before leaving the room. Togichi served the dinner for him and played the flute while the rest of the crew dined. The meal was small and not very good, but no one minded, for soon they were all seasick. Martin described the *Snark* at sea as the "plaything of the waves." He could not walk on deck without first securing two handholds for every step. If he didn't do so, he unwittingly became an aerial acrobat as the boat tossed him back and forth.

In addition to the seasickness, the crew soon had other troubles. The bathroom broke, and more severely, the whole boat leaked. The specially picked Puget Sound wood of which the *Snark* was built proved to be full of holes. Water spilled into food supplies, including fresh oranges, apples, carrots, turnips, beets, and cabbages, spoiling three months' worth of food. Seawater soaked and rusted their tools. Martin began wearing tall boots to keep his pants from soaking in the water. He cooked, but he could not bring himself to eat.

On top of all this, the *Snark*'s engine didn't work very regularly. The dynamo, meant to power nineteen electric lights and a searchlight, would not start, and the smell of gasoline filled the cabins. Their coal supply had spilled from its bags, limiting the crew to kerosene lamps. A week into the expedition, things were no better. A strong gale that Martin likened to "going down . . . the steep incline of a Roller-Coaster" took the boat's jib and staysail.

Whether out of the spirit of adventure or sheer stubbornness, the *Snark* and its crew continued to sail across the Pacific Ocean when others might have turned back to the safety of San Francisco Bay. "Life that lives is life successful," London told Martin. "The achievement of a difficult feat is successful adjustment to a sternly exacting environment."

Despite its leaks, the *Snark* was swift and straight. No one needed to hold the wheel to keep the boat on course, but each crew member kept watch for two hours at a time. On May 5, Martin finally felt some enjoyment in the trip. He wrote in his diary: "I've come to the point where I've forgotten what the world was like. The past is all like some dream. Our world is a big, blue expanse of water, reaching in an eternal circle to the horizon; a blue, clear-looking sky overhead, in which journeys the hot, glowing sun; and a tiny boat, a speck in the immensity of things, pursuing its solitary way across the deep."

As the crew grew more comfortable with life at sea, they began to watch the ocean, and troublingly, they noticed a lack of wildlife. London felt that if they were on the right course, they should be seeing dolphin and fish, but there were none. While this worried them, they sailed on, each member of the crew pursuing his own interests during the long hours at sea. London wrote for two hours every morning, and Togichi read Japanese novels and did laundry off the back of the boat. Everyone bathed in the ocean while never letting go of the boat, except for Bert, who was a strong swimmer Martin likened to "a young Hercules." The men relaxed into an outfit of bare chests, white trousers, and canvas shoes. They all took pictures, including Martin, who began developing all their photos in the cabin's makeshift darkroom. They also played cards and listened to music on the phonograph London had brought on board along with a selection of more than five hundred records. London had also brought along an "Edison language-machine," which taught foreign languages with sound and textbooks. Thus, the *Snark* was filled with instrumental music and opera, as well as beginning Italian, German, Spanish, and French on an otherwise silent ocean.

On May 6 they crossed into the Tropics, and for a full week they did not encounter another ship. London saw a strange white bird he did not recognize, prompting him to take the navigation tools from Roscoe. By London's calculations, they were some fourteen miles off course, but the crew could not make the *Snark* heave-to. That is, they could neither slow it down nor hold its direction. "I realize now, that, joking aside, this is as perilous a voyage as ever human beings voluntarily ventured on," Martin reflected in his diary. "We could never weather a hard storm."

All the books they read said there should be fish in these waters, but there were still very few. This worried them. After a week of trying to get back on track, the crew began to doubt Roscoe's navigation skills even more. "[I] don't think anyone knows our bearings within one hundred miles or so," suspected Martin. On May 13 Roscoe claimed they were a little over a week from Hawaii, but at night the stars looked unfamiliar. Soon, however, they began to see signs of life. Flying fish and a large pod of rare finback whales swam by. At dusk three days later, they saw their first land since leaving California.

During Martin's usual four to six a.m. shift, he looked up into a sky filled with clouds. London joined him on deck, and the two wondered if what they thought was land the night before were only clouds on the horizon. Discouraged, they watched the sun rise. As the sun climbed above the horizon, London and Martin realized they had been right after all. Between parting clouds they spied land. It was the peak of Mauna Loa, Hawaii's 13,679-foot-tall active volcano—the largest in the world.

The *Snark* was within twenty-five miles of Pearl Harbor, but there was no wind. In fact, what little wind there was, was blowing the anxious crew away from Hawaii and toward the island of Molokai, where there was a leper colony. Leprosy, not completely understood at the time, was widely believed to be spread by even the slightest contact, so if the crew landed at Molokai, they were likely to be quarantined. Fortunately, a tugboat saw them floundering and approached, towing them into Pearl Harbor. When word of the famous American adventurers, long imagined lost at sea, reached the island, two boats from the Hawaiian Yacht Club came to meet them. It was May 20. The crew finally stepped on land once again, greeted, much as they had disembarked, by crowds of reporters and photographers.

Hawaii was a mixture of familiar and exotic. At the end of the nineteenth century, the United States annexed Hawaii, in part to secure the thriving sugar industry. After agitating for the overthrow of the monarchy, the United States set up a provisional government, and American businesses moved into the territory.

A young Martin sits aboard the *Snark* during his first South Seas adventure. (Courtesy of California State Parks)

When the *Snark* arrived, Hawaii was in the process of being Westernized but still contained an eclectic mixture of native Hawaiian, Asian, and American cultures. Unfamiliar flat-bottomed Japanese boats, known as sampans, filled the harbor, and the streets of Pearl City were lined with bungalows and gardens. Martin marveled at the healthy island gardens filled with "plenty of food, growing right to one's hand." "[N]o tropical diseases to be seen," he continued, "at least not yet; no dirt, no smoke; everything so pleasing and satisfying as to be beyond description." The idyllic scene was marred only by mosquitoes. Martin found his days filled with leisure after the crew revolted against his cooking and began dining with local families. "[T]he poor, harassed crew forgot its troubles in the delight of eating once more the things that humans eat, cooked as humans would cook them," Martin acknowledged self-deprecatingly.

The crew received curious visitors on board the *Snark*. Americans, British, Japanese, and Hawaiians all wanted a glimpse of the strange little ship that had sailed from California—and of the famous writer who had led the expedition. Newspapers reported London "was a big, bullyragging brute, and had beaten [the crew] into a pulp," said Martin, asserting such reports were absolutely untrue. "[T]here was never so much as a quarrel among us," he avowed.

After a while, the Londons went to Honolulu, leaving Martin in Pearl City to watch the boat. London sent film back from the city, which Martin would develop and return to Honolulu via the mile-long railroad between the two cities. He befriended the train conductor, Tony, who went out of his way to pick fresh fruit for the *Snark* crew and didn't charge them for their deliveries. Eventually, Martin found his chance to visit Honolulu, and Tony gave him a free ride. Once in Honolulu, Martin and London tried their luck at the native sport of surfing. "[I] was nearly drowned," Martin divulged, "and managed to swallow a few quarts of salt water before the fun wore off." London had a bit more skill, but at the end of the day he was so sunburned he went directly to bed. Martin admitted surfing was something the native Hawaiians mastered while white men floundered, save a very few who had won local competitions. Martin stuck to swimming, fishing, and watching for underwater wildlife like large sea turtles, hammerhead sharks, and giant devil rays.

Meanwhile, the *Snark*'s crew began to disperse. Having proved his inability to navigate, Roscoe left on a steamship to return to the States. London hired a new captain, and while he was an experienced South Seas sailor, Martin thought him too "rough and headstrong." He and the captain butted heads early and did their best to ignore each other from then on. London also hired an engineer, Gene Fenelon, who had known London in Oakland. Fenelon was thirty years old and had worked as a manager of a European circus for eight years. He and Martin became good pals. The young men, working on cleaning the *Snark* and painting its galley, wore swim suits all day, and though they thought this uniform quite risqué, they noted that most people there wore even less. At night, Martin and Fenelon went to the Hawaiian Yacht Club for drinks and got so drunk that on their walk home, Martin said they "frighten[ed] the very birds off their perches by our vigorous sea-songs."

Meanwhile, London hired some men from Honolulu to help fix up the *Snark*. They got the dynamo running again and stopped the leaks. They also installed a new gas engine. Martin stayed with the boat while London and Charmian again left, this time to tour the other Hawaiian Islands. While alone, Martin would watch the night fall, the landscape bathed in moonlight. "In the harbor lay the *Snark*, looking as if lighted by electricity where the moonbeams were mirrored on her freshly painted sides and her polished metal," he reflected, "and further away was the shadowy shore-line, fringed by groves of cocoanut palms, and still further back, fading away into the night, were the majestic mountains." Martin was anxious to begin the rest of their journeys through the alluring South Sea islands.

Martin sailed the boat to Honolulu with the temperamental captain, Togichi, and Fenelon. The captain treated the crew badly, cursing at them so harshly that they refused to cooperate at all and let the captain crash the boat. Upon arriving in Honolulu, a furious Martin called London from the docks telling him he ought to fire the "profane captain." London took a cab from his hotel and did so immediately.

Again Honolulu impressed Martin with its streetcars and large American-style houses. It seemed a "veritable Paradise of the Pacific," mixing the beauty of the natural landscape with American improvements and the skilled gardening and landscaping of the Japanese. He hiked to the crater of an extinct volcano known as the Punch Bowl. In town, the Royal Hawaiian Band and Sunday school choirs of Japanese and Kanakas (the term used to refer to indentured Pacific Islanders) performed in native dress. "It was very enjoyable, even if we couldn't understand a word of their songs," wrote Martin. On the Fourth of July, a parade of fourteen thousand American troops walked through the city, and several soldiers played a game of baseball against a team of Japanese boys (the latter won).

London hired another captain and persuaded his longtime servant and friend Togichi to stay on. Togichi had experienced such severe seasickness that he was reluctant to continue. London postponed their departure several times as they prepared the boat, causing lighthearted ridicule from locals and newspapers. "When will the *Snark* sail?" called newsboys. "Not yet, but soon." When they finally did depart, they sailed from Honolulu slowly "as a boy would float a [boat]" for a week before pulling in to anchor in the shadow of the Big Island's Mauna Loa.

They sailed up the west coast of Hawaii to their next planned stop, Kailua (along what is now called the Kona Coast), "one of the most lonesome, desolate spots" Martin had ever seen. The crew forbid him to cook, and he often had free time. "I used to sit on the lava coast and try to see across the several thousand miles to America," he said, "where there were people to whom I could speak; I did not understand these people here." Martin and Togichi hiked along the coast and inland, visiting rice and coffee plantations. He marveled at the artificial marshes built by Chinese farmers for rice cultivation and at the artificial ponds that they stocked with fish. Before leaving, the entire crew hiked to the grave of the explorer Capt. James Cook, near the Kealakekua Bay in Kailua. A white pinnacle marked the spot where the first white man to visit the islands died in 1779, at the hands of native villagers. Though Cook had previously had peaceful relations with the Hawaiians, a squabble broke out over a stolen boat, and they clubbed him on the beach as he tried to depart.

When London and Charmian left the crew and rode horseback to Hilo, Togichi decided he had had enough. The seasickness was more than he could endure, so he boarded a steamer for California. Martin was sad to see him go. Martin, Fenelon, and the captain sailed the *Snark* around the island to meet the

Londons. From the water they saw towering waterfalls, luxurious vegetation, and ripening fruit trees all along the coast. When they stepped onto the beach at Hilo, Martin felt he had arrived in paradise: "[T]he damp sand was always cool and refreshing and the sea breeze blowing made one want to take off his shoes and roll up his trousers, and splash along in the water, a thing I did many a time. Truth is, people, after a few weeks in the Sandwich Islands, start doing things they would never think of doing in the staid old United States. The climate seems to make one younger, for it is always spring in Hawaii."

When London went diving at nearby Cocoanut Island, Martin accompanied him but remained on the island, where he met a native girl. She agreed to have her photograph taken, but the beach was too bright, so they walked to the shade of some trees where Martin took as many pictures as his film supply allowed. Martin admired the beauty of this native girl, but, lest he seem to be "going native," he explained that the islands' native girls were not "the only good-looking girls in Hilo. Some of the Japanese girls with whom I had a photographing acquaintance were as chic as are to be found any place. . . . [T]o see them gliding along," he revealed, "makes a man ashamed of his own uncouthness when he chances to meet one of them." One wonders if Martin, as a young man alone and free on an island of women he found so appealing, had more than a "photographing acquaintance" with some of them.

Fenelon accompanied Martin on trips up rivers and streams, collecting fruit that grew right along the banks. The young men spent so much time outdoors in just swimming trunks and sleeveless shirts that they became nearly blackened by the sun. Unfortunately for Martin, who enjoyed his company, Gene also decided to leave the expedition. The trip, he said, was proving too much for his "delicate constitution." London agreed Gene would have a hard time as they approached more rugged islands and promoted Martin to engineer. "I don't believe I would have traded positions with the President, or King Edward, that day," said Martin, much delighted. London also added an experienced Dutch sailor, Hermann; an English-speaking Japanese cook, Wada; and a Japanese cabin boy from Hilo, Nakata, who spoke no English. Martin thought Hermann (who never revealed his last name, as far as Martin knew) was "one of the real deep-water sailors, of the kind that is rapidly passing away. . . . He was about the best-natured fellow I ever worked with."

After five months on the Hawaiian Islands, the *Snark* again left port with a crowd of newly made friends to see them off. As the new crew sailed from Hilo across the "trackless Pacific" toward the Marquesas Islands, Martin peered at the ocean with anticipation for "the greatest adventurous event of my life." However, when they turned into open water, everyone was immediately seasick, except for Hermann, who grumbled that those with weak stomachs should not be so foolish as to take to the sea. They were now passing a section of the Pacific Ocean that people rarely, if ever, crossed. Those who had tried either disappeared or landed on the Samoan or Fiji islands instead of the Marquesas.

They passed the time with fishing contests and practicing harpooning dolphinfish from the boat. London even set aside his writing to join in the fun. There were thousands of fish and several species of shark. Soon, however, the sky darkened, and Martin thought if he had seen "such elemental disturbances [in Kansas], we should have hunted the storm-cellar." Storms set in for the next week, playing with the *Snark* like a toy, toppling it onto its side and pouring water onto its decks. The storm pushed them farther west than they would have liked.

For three weeks the boat moved swiftly on strong winds before reaching the Doldrums, where the winds died completely. Martin couldn't help but think of all the ships lost in this region. "A grim possibility stared us in the face," he admitted. "But all things come to those who dare," he declared, feeling braver with each adventure. London was clearly rubbing off on him. The Doldrums encircle the earth just north of the equator and had indeed trapped many a sailing expedition. It is there that winds from north and south meet, creating a calm in the middle of the ocean. Winds often come at random and from divergent directions, leaving sailboats floundering. To add to their anxiety about these unpredictable conditions, the crew discovered their water tank had been carelessly left open (no one would admit to the deed) and their main water supply depleted. London rationed the last ten gallons of water to a pint a day. Suffering of thirst, Martin felt the burning irony of the previous week's storms that now—when they needed fresh water—would not come. Turning misfortune into inspiration, London went into his cabin and wrote a story about a sailor who dies of thirst at sea. Fortunately for the crew, they did not succumb to that fate, for it rained the next day, and they collected enough water for the rest of their journey.

The *Snark* made it through the Doldrums and began to sail easily, with land 350 miles away. With Hermann confidently at the helm, the rest of the crew tried to improve their own navigation skills, played cards, and taught Nakata English. Martin developed more photographs and worked on the engine. During the contemplation of the expanses in which he found himself, Martin remembered it was one year ago that he had left his Kansas home.

When at last they reached the thatched-hut-lined coast of Nuka Hiva, the sight made Martin feel he was finally in the "real South Sea islands." Nuka Hiva, the largest island in the Marquesas chain, had a landscape that inspired at least two exemplary adventure writers—Herman Melville and Robert Louis Stevenson. "We dared mightily," Martin said, proud of making it through. "We did the impossible. We cheated the chances, we defeated the odds that lay against us." Around midnight they pulled into the narrow port of Taiohae Bay in the southern part of the island, leaving a squall on the sea for the beauty of the bay that was, on all sides, surrounded by mountains. "It seems that we must be in paradise," said Martin. "The air is perfume."

The *Snark* was greeted by natives offering fruit and, when they heard the crew was headed to the Typee Valley, asking to be hired as guides. Melville had made the Typee Valley immortal in his first novel, *Typee* (1846). The author had been held captive on Nuka Hiva, and his book was based on his life among the natives. "[F]or years and years," claimed Martin, "in fact, since he was a little boy . . . Jack had longed to visit" this spot. London wanted to know if Melville's descriptions of the island paradise were true or romanticized. Martin was immediately captivated by the island's charms, luxurious vegetation, and "sweet flowers." The captain of another ship in port helped them arrange for horses and good guides into the legendary valley. On horseback, they ascended precipitous mountain paths to a peak from which they could see down into several valleys, home to many different tribes. "[W]e found," said Martin, "that Melville had told the truth—that if he had not told the whole truth, it was because he had not described all the beauties of this bewitching valley of leisure and abundance. . . ."

They rode farther through forests of wild bananas and coconuts, and arrived at the ruined village of Typee. Coconut trees were arranged in a curious circle, as Melville had described, but natives no longer lived there. Only lepers, who lived in an old trader's cabin, made the valley home. The *Snark* crew continued to search for the powerful people who had held Melville captive over a half century ago. Farther along, they found twenty grass houses that were home to somewhere between fifty and seventy-five natives, apparently all that was left of the tribe that had numbered at least six thousand by Melville's account. Wars with other tribes and disease brought by missionaries and traders (including leprosy, elephantiasis, and venereal disease) had decimated the once-mighty people. "My conscience smote me," reflected Martin. "To think, the very pennies I had given in Sunday School for foreign missions had contributed to the calamitous end of the inhabitants of this beautiful garden-spot!" Travel was expanding his horizons and beginning to challenge his provincial Kansas upbringing. What he had been told about the South Seas was tested by his newfound experiences.

The natives welcomed the visitors with a meal of raw fish, poi (mashed taro root), eggs, chicken, and coconuts, which they served on the ruins of a stone house. They entertained their guests with music, dancing, and singing. "I could not help thinking of my friends at home," thought Martin, "who were bundled in heavy clothes, trying to keep warm, and going to moving-picture shows and dances, and persuading themselves that they were really having a pleasant time." Martin's increasing distance from American life instilled in him little desire to return to it—both its entertainment and the system that had destroyed this island's fascinating people and culture.

The next day, Martin tried to photograph their curious method of tattooing but found he could not capture it with his camera no matter which exposure he tried. The natives were interested in the phonograph, which London had brought along to intrigue them. Two hundred natives from all around the valley came to listen to what they imagined was a dwarf trapped in a box. London played familiar tunes, like the Hawaiian hula-hula, and the people danced. They created dances to music less familiar as well, leading Martin to conclude: "A Polynesian can no more keep from dancing when he hears music than a duck can keep away from water."

After two weeks on Nuka Hiva, the *Snark* was again ready to set sail. The Typee Valley had been everything they had dreamed of, a veritable "Garden of Eden . . . if ever there was [one]." The climate, the fruit, the mountain- and waterfall-filled landscape, the wild game and birds, and the native people—all were wild yet unafraid. Humans and nature lived, it seemed to Martin, "a life of perfect peace." As they prepared to leave, Martin looked again at the panorama of mountains in Taiohae Bay: "Photographs give no idea of its beauty. And I know no description can do it justice. . . . Very often, when lost in admiration of its beauty, I have

Dressed in the native attire of the Solomon Islands, Martin looks healthy, but the bandage on his right leg covers a festering sore.

experienced a pang of regret that a scene so enchanting should be hidden from the world in these remote seas, and seldom meet the eyes of devoted lovers of nature." London's plan to write a full report about the people of the South Seas never materialized, but Martin's own desire to bring the landscapes and cultures of the region to American audiences had been stirred.

At the end of the week, they docked in Papeete Bay on the island of Tahiti. Martin dubbed this capital of French Polynesia the "Paris of the South Sea islands." The bay was filled with pearl divers' boats dwarfed by two warships—one American and the other French. American sailors cheered and saluted as the *Snark* pulled in. They had been expecting the ship for months. A canoe approached them with a native paddler and a white man dressed only in a loincloth who offered them jars of honey and jam. As Martin soon found out, this was an acquaintance of London's named Ernest Darling, whose eccentric ways earned him the nickname the "Nature Man." Ernest had trouble with pneumonia and something American doctors described as "overstudy" (most likely a nervous breakdown brought on by stress). When they tried to put him in an asylum, he protested and found refuge in Tahiti, where the French let him live as he pleased. He strongly believed in a natural, vegetarian diet, and there he had all the fresh fruit he desired.

The Society Islands are a chain of twenty-five islands, of which Tahiti is biggest. Papeete had the largest population in Polynesia at the time, with full-time residents numbering about five thousand. French, Chinese, and native Polynesians made up the majority, but there were some New Zealanders, Australians, Germans, and Americans, as well. The town sat at the base of the mountains, and just outside were expansive coconut groves and sugar plantations. There were several French-looking business buildings and modern streets. French "bungalows" were landscaped with neat lawns, ferns, and palms, but native grass houses remained in town, as well.

Martin befriended the American soldiers who showed him the town. They liked to watch the strange mix of goods unloaded off trade schooners, which carried everything from pearl shells to live turtles. Mostly, however, what the soldiers and Martin had in common was an interest in women. "I think Papeete might easily be called the city of girls," gushed Martin, "for they outnumber the male population two to one." Native girls entertained in the streets with accordion music and dancing. Every night was carnivalesque to Martin, to whom "the streets seem to be flooded with nothing but girls."

During their time in Papeete, London fired the Dutch sailor Hermann for a particularly bad drunken episode. Soon thereafter, the *Snark*'s progress was further stalled by news from home. A financial panic had hit the United States, and London felt he had to return to take care of his finances. With regrets and promises to return, he and Charmian left on the steamer *Mariposa* for California, leaving the rest of the crew on the island. "No one was sorry that we were delayed," said Martin, "for we had just about decided that we should like to live here."

And so they did, at least for a while. Martin hired men to help fix the *Snark*'s still troublesome engine and enjoyed afternoons hiding from the heat in a rented bungalow shared with the captain. They spent some days doing nothing but eating tropical fruit, drinking absinthe and cognac, and smoking. Native girls came to their house and showed them the "real hula-hulas." Several of Papeete's private clubs had extended membership to London and his crew, so Martin and the captain went out nights for dancing and more drinking. Martin remembered this luxurious — if not somewhat debaucherous — lifestyle when he returned to the States: "Now that I am back in America, I can appreciate their quiet lazy life better than I could then. To be able to sit or sleep under those big shady trees or to take a book out there to read, all the time with plenty of fruit handy, and with nothing to worry over, is a genuine luxury."

During this time, Martin befriended a native woman named Helene who lived on the island of Raiatea and had some influence over traders at Papeete. He met her in the marketplace, where she boldly grabbed his hand and greeted him with a "hello, missionary," in her native language. The captain explained to her, as he understood the language, that they were not missionaries. Helene seemed pleased and told Martin he could buy her and her friends fruit and flowers. He did. When he ran into her again, she greeted him with "hello," but "she no longer called me missionary, nor was I ever called missionary again. I'm sure I never gave any of them cause to mistake me for a missionary; in fact, after the crew of the *Snark* had become acquainted in Papeete, I'm afraid the real missionaries did not approve of our keeping open house to the natives."

Helene began visiting the bungalow every day, and Martin soon learned that her mother was sick. He lent her money for medicine, and in exchange, she brought him watermelons. Through her, he learned some of the Tahitian language. Martin took her along on photographing trips in a rented buggy. He told her of life in America, "of circuses, of trains, of tall skyscrapers," and watched her face light up when he took her to the movies at the Folies Bergere theater on Saturday evenings. There, cities and railroads danced across the screen, and "it was many a day before the natives [like Helene] could understand that it was not supernatural."

After three and a half months, Jack and Charmian returned to Tahiti, and the crew prepared to sail for Raiatea "on a special invitation from Helene." They were all excited to see the island, which was free of any Western cultivation and in a "wild natural state." Ernest Darling and a socialist friend came along, as well as a new hire, an eighteen-year-old Frenchman named Ernest, and a Tahitian navigator named Tehei. When the *Snark* pulled into Moorea Bay, natives swam out to the boat and played with its electric lights. Martin took some girls out in the launch "to their most frantic pleasure." London gave the crew nights off while at Raiatea, and each night they anchored there, Martin would take the launch to shore and walk up the mountain to Helene's home. Though her parents welcomed him, they did not seem to have the confident air she possessed, and Martin wondered how she had grown so powerful among the traders at Papeete if not by birthright or upbringing. "[I]t must have been," he thought, "some strength of character, some intrinsic worth that elevated her in station and in mind."

After four days, the *Snark* sailed through a channel of coral reefs to Tahaa and Bora Bora. "This," proclaimed Martin, "was the real South Seas that I had read about, dreamed about, and had never expected to see." Native canoes paddled up to them, and many, curious about the unusual ship and crew, tried to climb on board. With local navigator Tehei along, they were hosted by royalty at Bora Bora, where his wife and her family ruled. The whole island organized to entertain and prepare a feast for the visitors. Bora Bora was a wild island thick with vegetation, and the people seemed wild, too, playing what Martin called "barbarous tunes" and dancing "so strange and indescribable as to arouse the disbelief of some who have never traveled in the South Seas." Yet Martin admired their seemingly carefree life, preferring it to that of so-called civilization. In the morning, a bugle from a conch shell woke them, and they found several canoes pulled up onto the beach. One double canoe contained fourteen young women, the "belles of Bora Bora," Martin called them. He went down in the launch with his camera and took photographs of the scene. London teased him for being so girl crazy and asked him if he wished he were in the boat with the fourteen beauties. "[H]e was getting the better of me," thought Martin, "until I ran alongside and three of the girls jumped in the launch, after which I sped on, with the laugh on Jack."

Indentured native servants, known as Kanakas, canoed up to see the *Snark*, as well. Kanakas were native Polynesians who were mostly kidnapped for the slave trade (or "blackbirded") within the British colonies. Martin invited them on board and showed them the engine room in exchange for watermelons. He demonstrated electricity by shocking one with live wires. The friendly natives were amazed at such strange technology. Martin further amazed them when he repaired a clock in the royal house, while London impressed them with his phonograph. They spent ten days there, and when they left, the natives shook their hands and filled the boat with food. "Our hearts' roots seemed to have found grateful soil in Bora Bora," Martin reflected. "The place is a happy paradise; and the life is one to envy. Everything seems to work for good to the natives."

In mid-April, the crew was back at sea, sailing toward the Samoan Islands. Martin painted and polished the engine room and practiced his boxing moves with London. Charmian had purchased a ukelele and played while Tehei, Wada, and Nakata danced.

They all spent hours jumping rope, playing cards, and, oddly, spinning tops. "I have seen Jack London squat down and spin his tops by the hour," marveled Martin, "thoroughly absorbed in the fun. He said that this, like his cigarettes, soothed his nerves."

In the heat of the afternoon, London read them some of the articles on which he had been working: "The Chinago" (set in Papeete), "The Seed of McCoy," and "The Other Animals." The latter was London's response to accusations from American colleagues, namely explorer-president Theodore Roosevelt and nature-writer John Burroughs, who had accused London of anthropomorphizing animals, calling him a "nature faker," a name he took as the worst of insults to his work.

After thirteen days sailing west, they saw the peaks of the Manua Islands, a group of the Samoas. They sailed near shore but could not find a path through the coral reefs. Martin gazed at the shores, where he could make out grass-hut villages backed by dark jungles that contrasted in light and color with the bright blues of the ocean. A group of natives came out to greet them in a whale boat and towed the *Snark* past the reefs. Jack and Charmian went on shore, but the rest stayed behind to clean the boat. When his duties were done, Martin bribed a native with tobacco to shuttle him to shore. As they were paddling in, however, the canoe sank, and Martin swam to shore to the sound of laughing natives. They took him to the king and queen's house where London and Charmian were and told the story to everyone. They all laughed and shook hands. The king offered his guests a kava drink (which has a sedative effect) in coconut shells and made a toast. He fed them a dinner of unfamiliar dishes and traded curios—war clubs, tapa cloth, mats, and fans.

From the Manuas, the *Snark* continued to Pago Pago on the Samoan island of Tutuila, which Martin thought "the prettiest land-locked harbour I have ever seen." It was surrounded by mountains, and villages dotted its shores. Martin's enthusiasm was getting the best of him—every new place they visited became his favorite. The South Seas was endearing itself to him. Pago Pago was home to an American military station with some three hundred soldiers stationed there, some with native wives, and all living the leisurely life of the islands Martin had come to admire. The soldiers held parties and balls, read literature, and even had a baseball diamond. The *Snark* crew spent a week there, during which time London fired Ernest and hired another sailor, Henry—a six-foot-tall "mountain of muscle" who knew navigation and many European and native languages.

The *Snark* sailed on to Apia, where they explored the ruins of a city and a German schooner wrecked there in an 1889 hurricane. The island was home to five thousand Germans and natives who had erected buildings around the bay of "white coral cement, showing up like white marble from the sea." But their real interest in Apia was in Robert Louis Stevenson's home, Villa Vailima, where he spent the last years of his life writing his South Seas stories. Stevenson's house sat on a hillside below his writing pagoda and grave, perched at the top of the mountain.

As the *Snark* sailed away from Apia, the crew looked back to the island on which it sat, Upolu, and saw a volcano emitting fire and oozing lava down its sides like "threads that grew into glowing torrents as we came closer, until by midnight we were sailing up the coast of an island that seemed to be literally aflame." Lava flowed into the ocean, and steam rose from the water. Curious about this phenomenon, the crew took the temperature of the water and found it to be near boiling point. Thinking of the gasoline on board, they quickly turned the boat away. Henry had wanted to take them to a village on the island but now wondered if the village still existed. "By the light of the boiling lava we could see ruined villages and hundreds of thousands of naked cocoanut trees," described Martin, "stripped of their foliage and standing straight and threadbare in the fiery glow, like trimmed poles."

They watched the display through the night and in the morning saw a village that looked unharmed. The *Snark* anchored, and

London, Charmian, and Martin went to shore on the launch. Women were praying outside a church, pleading for protection from the oozing volcano. The governor of the town was an Irishman, Dick Williams, who invited the crew to stay with him overnight. In the morning he took them closer to the eruption. They walked precipitously on dried lava and watched slow flows moving down the mountainside. They stuck coins onto the ends of sticks, dipping them into the lava to make souvenirs. For five days they explored the volcanic activity near this town, called Matautu. Martin wanted to get even closer to the source, but the native who guided him to the crater forced him to turn back. "I got to within half a mile of the crater," he said, "but near enough to see the awful yawning hole, nearly a mile across, emitting thousands and thousands of tons of liquid death every minute."

After experiencing the South Seas' volatile landscape, they were all rather glad to be back at sea, where the familiar dangers of reefs and drenching gales seemed tame by comparison. They made their way through the Ringgold Islands toward the Koro Sea—a two-hundred-mile lagoon encircled by islands. They were met by another boat that turned out to be that of a trader, Frank Whitcomb, who was a big fan of London's books. He came on board the *Snark* to visit with, in his opinion, "the greatest man that ever lived."

The *Snark* then docked at Suva, a cosmopolitan British town in Fiji where the streets were filled with a colorful mix of native Fijians, Hindus, and British. Jack and Charmian stayed at a posh hotel, thought to be the most famous in the whole South Seas, run by a Mrs. McDonald. Inland, the island was filled with "primitive life." Martin joined an excursion across the bay that took him up streams into mango swamps and native villages. The *Snark* made the final leg of its journey to the islands of the New Hebrides (now Vanuatu). There, Martin found the native people even more intriguing. "They can scarcely be written about in language sufficiently plain to give a definite idea of them," he wrote. "The hundred or more pictures I made of these cannibals cannot be printed in a volume intended for popular circulation," he regretted. Martin regretted more not being able to prove the peoples' cannibalism. Their clothing—what there was of it—was "designed solely for purposes of suggestion." They seemed possessed of a different morality, thought Martin, who called them "sex worshippers" but gave no details other than their scanty dress. The women wore grass skirts with lifted bustles that Martin thought quite odd. He wondered, jokingly, if the bustle of Western dress was inspired by the dress of these natives. "I fully expect," he continued, "to see some day the prettiest ladies of our land wearing enormous nose-rings, as there are places in the world where such nose-rings constitute the entire wardrobe."

As the *Snark* pulled into the island of Tanna, the contrast to the welcoming Polynesian native lifestyle was further brought into focus by a group of ragged, dirty natives boarding the ship and stealing anything they could carry. On the island, the crew had dinner with a missionary, Reverend Watt, whom Martin thought "a fairly decent sort of man" but did not approve of his methods of conversion of natives. Watt refused to take them into the island's interior, explaining that he worked only with coastal natives and feared those who lived farther inland. It was certainly, he said, eyeing Charmian, "no place for a woman!"

In addition to the feared inland natives, Watt warned them to steer clear of a certain trader, called Wiley. London immediately whispered to Martin that they must find this man, and it would be easier than they thought. When they returned to the *Snark*, he was on board waiting for them, comfortably helping himself to London's cigarettes. Martin thought he was friendly and wondered why the missionary did not like him. Wiley explained that he made friends with natives by doctoring them, which angered Watt, who used healing medicines to gain the faith and loyalty of native peoples, a technique common to mission conversions. Thus, they had been butting heads for years.

Wiley offered to take them into the interior of the island. On the day scheduled, however, Wiley was sick, so his partner, Frank Stanton, guided them instead. He took them to a village where, three years before, he had seen a cannibal feast, reported to be the last one that ever took place in the South Seas. The native men of the village wore only belts and were covered by tattoos and paint—a condition London described as "worse than naked." Their hair was dyed red and tied back with coconut fiber. They wore anklets and necklaces of porpoise teeth and shell, and had large wooden rings through their pierced ears, which were distended from the weight of the adornments. Women wore just a leaf on a string around their waists, to conceal their genitalia, and a good share of jewelry. Martin took photographs of these people, mustering as much calmness as he could. When they returned to the boat, Martin breathed a sigh of relief, feeling his first gut resistance to a culture so different from his own. "I had been far from comfortable among these ferocious-looking bush people," he revealed.

Having seen their share of native life for the moment, when the volcano on Tanna began to rumble and smoke, they decided to explore this natural phenomenon instead. They found a guide to lead them to an overlook from which they peered down into the crater's bubbling and boiling lakes of molten lava.

After a week, the *Snark* set sail again. The waters were calm, but volcanoes seemed to be smoking or spewing all around them. Soon, they came to a remote Solomon Island where natives in canoes quickly surrounded the *Snark*, shouting at them and raising spears, clubs, and bows threateningly. They held the people at bay with guns, noticing their unusual jewelry made of tin sardine cans and teacup handles, which they had acquired from traders and put to new, imaginative uses. Their teeth had been filed down and were jet black, and their lips were bright red. They all had tattoos of "monstrous designs." After a while, a man came out in a canoe. When he stood up to say hello and attempted a formal bow, he toppled out of the canoe and into the ocean. Everyone laughed, and the man climbed on board the *Snark*. He told the crew that despite the standoff, the people on the island were friendly, and he would take them ashore if they liked.

London, Charmian, and Martin went on shore, where they were greeted by women wearing only jewelry and a string of beads around their waists. While there they met a trader, Tom Butler, whose partner, he told them, had been killed by the inland people for food, confirming that cannibals still existed in the region and that the tribes there were headhunters, as well. Cannibalism, Martin learned, was not a tradition practiced because of sheer brutality or perverse taste for human flesh. Rather, the natives believed eating human meat gave one the power and strength of the dead man. White men were particularly vulnerable to being killed for this ritual, he learned, because of the technologies they possessed that gave them a power the natives did not fully understand. While the crew did not see a cannibal feast on the island, they "saw plenty of evidence of the practice in the thousands of human bones on shores and reefs."

An English-speaking native led them to a village while one hundred natives followed from behind. They crossed a bridge that they forbid Charmian from stepping on, as it was taboo for women. Determined to go on, she waded across the water instead. "Poor Mrs. London was humiliated," Martin noticed, "but Jack enjoyed it."

Martin saw many gruesome and astonishing things on this island. Obscene figures were carved into totem poles. Headhunters had strewn shrunken heads in one area; London studied them while Martin took photographs. The corpse of a recently deceased king was placed in a coffin and stuck through with arrows, meant to drain supposedly poisonous elements from the body. These arrows were then used by the people as weapons. Gruesome as it was, Martin purchased 150 of the poisoned arrows. Even the living people were grisly. Two men they encountered were victims of shark attacks. One had his entire leg bitten off, while the other's leg had "all the flesh stripped from the bone." Through the lens of his camera, Martin confronted these atrocities and made a record of these unbelievable sights.

Though they had no specific injuries to cause them, Martin and London soon suffered from flesh-eating sores on their feet. No medicine seemed to work, and a doctor was thousands of miles away. Martin's ankle and leg were swollen to double their normal size. Butler called these sores "yaws" and said it was quite common for white men in the Solomons to get them. The only thing he knew to help was to pour corrosive sublimate (mercuric chloride)—a toxic substance used to treat syphilis—on them. "It burnt like fire," admitted Martin, "but it seemed to help."

Having their fill of cannibal life and worrying about their worsening sores, the crew sailed on to Ugi, six miles farther. When they reached the shores, missionaries and traders marveled at their experiences on the "dark islands" and shared their own tales. The *Snark* then pushed on to Guadalcanal, where they were guests on the largest plantation, Penduffryn, run by two Englishmen named George Darbishire and Thomas Harding. While London rested and tried to recover from his ailments, Martin befriended a crew of French filmmakers from Pathe Freres—a motion picture company in Paris. The crew was on their way to film native cannibals and had been delayed by illness. More crucially, however, their film chemicals had been ruined by the heat and humidity. Martin offered some from his stock. The filmmakers were so grateful that they asked if he wanted to come along. Martin accepted, accompanying them to a village six miles inland, where he experienced motion-picture creation for the first time.

Meanwhile, Charmian fell ill. She remained at Penduffryn while London and Martin sailed the *Snark* to Tulagi, about twenty-five miles away, where they hiked an extinct volcano. London returned to Penduffryn to be with Charmian, leaving Martin to sail the *Snark* back. He joined the Londons, where card games and dancing seemed to last for days. The merriment ended when they all agreed to try hashish. The drug made London "clear off his head," and he "acted so wild," Martin said, "that Mrs. London was frightened." After that, no one had any interest in the drug.

Martin spent his days working on the *Snark* and developing photographs before rowing the launch in for dinner on the island. But once again, the crew was falling to pieces. London's and Martin's sores were not healed, and Henry, Tehei, and Nakata all had ailments. "I was looking forward to getting out of this particular part of the world," Martin admitted. "It was too wild and raw, too full of sickness and sudden death. How I longed for a real bed, with sheets, in a place where it was not too hot to sleep!" Then, London's hands and feet mysteriously began to swell. No one could figure out what it was. "It is plain we are not wanted in the South Seas," London told Martin, discouraged at the attack of the region's diseases. "California is the place for me." "And me for Kansas," Martin agreed.

From Guadalcanal, they took a steamer to Sydney, Australia, arriving there on November 15, 1907. The city, with street cars rumbling up the main thoroughfares, seemed rather American to Martin, who was happy to see familiar buildings and people once more. He went to the theater and dinner with Jack and Charmian, but they were both feeling ill and checked themselves into the hospital the next day. Martin had his sores treated but did not rest as he was told. He began running a fever and ended up in the hospital, as well,. London's swelling would not go away and puzzled the doctors. "I shall have to give up my voyage around the world," he told Martin with regret. "I can assure you that I am not a bit happy over all this."

When Martin was feeling better, London sent him back to Guadalcanal to retrieve the *Snark*. Martin hired a captain and, reunited with Tehei and Henry, began to sail the boat toward Sydney. As they sailed past the islands of Belonna and Rennell, two islands they had earlier hoped to visit, Martin wished he could stop and go ashore. He had heard the people were "the most primitive in the world—no stranger has ever reported setting foot ashore here." They sailed close to Rennell, and some of the natives came aboard. Even Henry could not understand their language, but they seemed to be inviting them to their village. The captain, however, would not allow it. Martin took photographs and gave them tobacco, which they spit right out. It was true, he thought, that these people remained unmarred by the outside world. Martin's interest in the cultures of the South Seas was not satisfied, and he regretted the end of the journey: "And this is my last of the South Seas for perhaps a long time, perhaps forever."

When they reached Sydney, they bade farewell to London and Charmian. Still craving adventure, Martin wrote a letter to Theodore Roosevelt, whom he had heard was planning an expedition to the South American Amazon. Not hearing back from Roosevelt, at the end of March 1908, Martin left Sydney and traveled around Australia, visiting Melbourne, Adelaide, Perth, and Hobart. He then began to make his way home, albeit slowly, using the money London had paid him. He traveled through the Indian Ocean to Ceylon, through the Arabian Sea to Aden, and through the Red Sea, by way of the Suez Canal, to Port Said. Once there, he tried again to communicate with Roosevelt, but the Roosevelt-Rondon Expedition had already begun its journey. Martin then toured Europe, stopping in Naples, Rome, Pompeii, and Paris. He stayed in Paris for a while, working as an electrician at the new amusement park, Luna Park. Feeling homesick, he crossed the English Channel to England and stowed away on a cattle boat from Liverpool to Boston in September. As he headed to America, Martin realized he was the only member of the *Snark* crew to complete their planned journey around the world. His health, endurance, perseverance, amiability—and perhaps a bit of just plain luck—proved he was appropriately groomed for a life of adventure.

CHAPTER 2

Honeymoon with Cannibals

It is a yearning—a yearning to get away from all this back here and be out in the great wild. It is the unfathomable unknown, the insoluble wilderness, that lures me.

— Martin Johnson

Women can stand the life of adventure just as well as any man . . . in the tropics anywhere on earth I would not be afraid to go alone and would come out healthier than while living in our so-called civilization.

— Osa Johnson

Martin had been away for three years when, in 1909, he returned home, welcomed by a brass band backed by a massive display of flags. His father, John, had kept the Kansas community up-to-date on their hometown adventurer by publishing Martin's letters in the local newspaper. If Martin hadn't realized he "had made it" as an adventurer, this hometown welcome proved he had. With such local interest in his travels, Martin rented a theater in town,

Martin stands outside his Snark Theater in Independence, Kansas, where he told the story of his adventures.

which he called "The Snark," and lectured about his travels using the photographs he took in the South Seas.

To add to the entertainment value of his lecture, Martin employed a young woman named Gail Perigo to complement his photographs with Hawaiian and Polynesian songs and dances. One night, Gail's sixteen-year-old friend Osa Leighty came to see her perform. Osa was so repulsed by the photographs of naked native people on display, she left the theater. Gail introduced her to Martin after the show, and Osa thought the young man quite full of himself. She told him point blank that she thought it was awful to show people the ugliness of cannibals. "I let him see I thought him conceited," said Osa, "and that I didn't think he had anything to be conceited about."

Like Martin, Osa Leighty was raised in Kansas. She was born on March 14, 1894, in Chanute to William Sherman Leighty, an engineer for the Santa Fe Railroad, and Ruby Isabelle Holman Leighty. Osa attended public school in Chanute and Sunday school at the Presbyterian church. Each summer, she went to stay at her grandparents' farm where Osa rode horses and nurtured her love of wide open spaces.

Though she had not yet exercised her sense of adventure, Osa had two strong role models who encouraged what would soon become her life's work. One of her grandmothers, Nancy Ann Wingfield Taylor (whom she called Winifred), had traveled West in a covered wagon train to Kansas and made her home on a rugged frontier still alive with constant Indian raids. Her grandmother's pioneer spirit would comfort Osa when she went to wild places. Her second role model, her Aunt Minnie—a rider in a traveling rodeo circuit—inspired Osa's daring and showmanship. When she was seven years old, Osa became known throughout the state for a performance at the William's Opera House in which she and a classmate dressed as an African-American boy and girl and danced the cake walk. Their performance earned them the title of Kansas's best cake walkers (an unofficial title, to be sure). Osa also won prizes for roller skating and, at ten years old, began singing at silent movies.

When Gail fell ill, Osa took her place at the Snark Theater despite her initial distaste for Martin Johnson and his photographs. Osa had decided she wanted to be an actress, so when the offer came to sing in the theater, she could not pass on the opportunity. By that time Martin had visited her in Chanute and had even met her parents, but Osa insisted they had nothing in common and that she had no interest in him. She still thought the young explorer was too prideful. To her surprise, Osa realized she must have had some interest in Martin when she thought she saw him flirting with another girl. Furious, she insisted on going to the station three hours before her train was due to depart for Chanute. Martin followed after her and proposed. They had known each other only a month, but something about his adventurous spirit and her natural glow in the spotlight drew them to one another.

They were married that same day, then boarded a train for Kansas City, Missouri, to be married again, hoping to prevent

Dressed in
Hawaiian costume,
Osa sang
alongside Martin's
presentation.

her parents from annulling the union as Osa, at sixteen and ten years younger than Martin, was legally underage to be wed in Kansas. After frantic phone calls with Osa's parents, they felt safe in returning to Chanute, though her irate father greeted Martin by telling him, "I never wanted to punch anybody so bad in my life."

Martin and Osa quickly became inseparable. Osa joined Martin's act permanently, and they briefly rented a flat in Independence before signing on to the vaudeville circuit, which sent them touring around the United States. Neither Martin nor Osa wrote much about this time in their lives, so little is known. They made friends with top performers with whom they shared billing, including Will Rogers and Chic Sale. Osa had never been outside of Kansas, and she no doubt found the experience exciting, even if

Osa sits atop a pile of luggage while she and Martin await a train in one of the many stations they visited on the vaudeville circuit.

they slept in mining camps, train stations, and wherever else their show was booked.

But giving lectures about his past travels only made Martin long for more adventure. It took them seven years, but as soon as they managed to save $4,000 from their earnings, they began to plan a trip to the South Seas, where Martin hoped to capture cannibal rituals on film. Before they left, Martin introduced Osa to Jack and Charmian London in California. Having heard Martin praise Charmian as "the best wife a man ever had," Osa paid careful attention to both her femininity and her ruggedness. The two women became good friends, and the Londons fully approved of Martin's chosen adventure-mate.

Charmian even sat by Osa's bedside when she was rushed to the hospital for emergency surgery. With her parents in Kansas and Martin in New York, Charmian stood in as Osa's guardian, approving a procedure for chronic appendicitis. When the doctors opened her up, however, they found more than an appendix problem. As Charmian wrote in a letter to Osa's mother, "her womb [was] upside-down, and pressing against her bowels so she had an incurable constipation." They also found a small cyst on her Fallopian tubes. If left untreated, they feared it would grow and require another more involved procedure in the future.

Because Osa was about to embark for the South Seas, where Charmian had experienced firsthand a lack of expert health care, Charmian told the doctors to do what they must. Ever curious, he watched the whole operation. The doctors removed the appendix and tumor, and fixed her uterus. "Osa, bless her dear little sweet soul, is now fixed for life," Charmian assured Osa's mother, Belle. "She will not have that awful constipation, she will have clearer skin, she'll get fat (she looked very thin to me) and she will have all kinds of better general health."

Charmian stayed with Osa until she came to, held her hand, and talked to her. Though she did not say it in so many words, from Charmian's description it seems clear that Osa's operation made her unable to conceive children. "There really was no good excuse not to have it all cleaned up now," Charmian said, assuring Osa and her mother that she was now "safe and sound" and that it was best this was done now if she were to travel with Martin. But her inability to have children haunted Osa for the rest of her life.

In the South Seas, Martin and Osa's limited funds kept them from getting distracted by every rumor and story of cannibalism they were told. Many people in Sydney reported former cannibal societies in the Solomon Islands, but Martin thought these people too tarnished by British colonialism. "They were subdued, tamed," he said of his experiences with them on the *Snark*. People wondered why he wouldn't simply stage the scenes he wanted using available native people—that's how others had done it. Osa was learning that Martin was not like the others, however. "Martin was a patient, persistent artist," she discovered, "who would never be satisfied with anything but the truth." She was starting to understand her husband's resolve.

Osa watched Martin work, asking questions and taking notes everywhere they went. After much investigation, he decided Malekula, one of the largest of the New Hebrides Islands, was the place to go. The island's size—seventy-five miles long by thirty miles wide—seemed to promise interior tribes unaffected by the outside world. Getting there, however, was another issue. One captain refused to drop them on the island, saying Maleku-lan cannibals were "ugly as the devil's own brats—and that's what they are, devils! Savage, cruel, murderous black devils!" Leaving a woman there, he said, would be pure murder. Everyone—trad-ers, missionaries, government officials—told them not to go. Even traders who had landed there would never think of doing so without some kind of backup. At the very least they would need an armed crew to protect them, these people insisted. "But I had the courage born of ignorance," Martin asserted, "and ventured boldly, taking it for granted that the tales told of the savages were wildly exaggerated."

The captain who refused to drop them at Malekula took them to the small neighboring island of Vao. The larger island of Malekula lay just southeast, but all the Johnsons could do was gaze toward the place they knew held their desired cannibals. Osa was frustrated and heartbroken that her presence was preventing them from reaching their destination. On Vao, they befriended a French missionary, Father Prin, who had succeeded in convert-ing only seventeen natives on the island of four hundred people. Osa admired the primitive church built of mud and grass, whose "quiet images and dim altar, seemed strange and beautiful on this savage island." Prin had a small house and invited them to rest there. He was a kind man, almost saintly, Martin thought. He had lived twenty-nine years in the South Seas, and while Martin was skeptical of missionaries, he respected this man's "grit . . . in a los-ing fight."

Prin told them what he knew of cannibalism among the people of Vao. He believed they hid their cannibalism out of

Martin cranks his motion picture camera to capture life at Ontong Java in the Solomon Islands.

fear of the British, but that they still practiced it. This made all the native activities seem more menacing. The native drums, or *boo-boos,* seemed to be signaling a potentially sinister ritual, and they wondered at the many faces peering curiously toward them. These were Osa's first encounters with South Seas natives, and she thought their pierced and contorted faces made it "hard to believe they were men at all." Seeing her initial repulsion, Martin said he would go to Malekula without her. She insisted he would most assuredly not. "If you go I'm going with you, Martin Johnson," she scolded. "That's what I came for and that's how it's going to be—the whole way. The whole way!"

Seeing their resolve, Father Prin finally conceded to help them get to Malekula. He gave them use of a whale boat, five men from Vao, and two Malekulan translators, and he blessed their journey from the beach. The most feared people on Malekula were a group of natives known as the Big Nambas (or "Big Numbers"), whose name referred to the large pandanus plant fibers they wore over their genitals. Traders, missionaries, and officials regarded their leader, Nagapate, as a "holy terror." The whole tribe was so feared that even neighboring people used them as a threat to misbehaving children. "The Big Nambas will get you!" was apparently a common reprimand of frustrated Malekulan parents.

Once they reached the island, Martin and Osa sailed north to Tanemarou Bay, where the Big Nambas resided. Some fierce-looking natives peered at their boat from the shore, then disappeared just as quickly as they had come. Martin and Osa landed on the sandy shore, and, though it looked deserted, they soon saw a native at the edge of the jungle. Even the Vao and Malekulan men who accompanied them backed away. "He was the most horrible looking creature I had ever laid eyes on," wrote Osa. His face was distorted, his hair greasy, and his body dirty. He wore a string of pig's teeth around his neck, a bone through his nose, and had pigtails hanging from his ears. He wore a pandanus fiber, confirming his identity as one of the Big Nambas. He approached and, in the broken language of the South Seas known as *Beche-de-Mer*, told Martin that his stomach hurt.

Martin had been warned many times about the dangers of giving out medicine. If something went wrong, the natives had a habit of blaming the Western drugs, even if the intentions were good. Martin, however, wishing to befriend these people, gave the man some pills and told him to save a few for later, but he took them all at once. Ten more Big Nambas men came to beach, and Martin set up his camera and began filming. He heard the men talking, and he thought they said Nagapate, the leader, was just inside the jungle watching their boat. Osa offered to go ahead with tobacco and calico as a peace offering, but Martin called her back. Osa kept walking, however, followed by the Malekulan and Vao men carrying trade goods and Martin's camera equipment. She was brave and not one to sit back when their opportunity was so near.

As she entered the tropical forest for the first time, Osa found the contrast disorienting. "After the glare of the beach," she marveled, "I seemed suddenly blind, and slid and stumbled along a dark trail that was treacherous with hidden muddy streams and wet creepers. The heavy, steaming breath of the swamps pressed down on us with the weight of something dead, and in it was the ominous smell of rot and slime." Despite her apparent lack of affection for the jungle, Osa kept walking, climbing a difficult uphill trail with Martin now following close behind. They climbed some three thousand vertical feet to the top of the mountain and emerged onto a sun-filled clearing from which they saw columns of smoke.

They rested for just a moment before a group of one hundred natives approached, four of them armed with guns. Martin and Osa tried to retreat peacefully, but the men raised their guns threateningly. Just then Nagapate came into view. "We knew without being told that this was Nagapate himself," Martin said, finding himself both afraid and respectful of the chief. Nagapate's figure was large and muscular, his jaw powerful, and his eyes intelligent. He wore four rings that seemed "to have come from the hands of his victims." He was, Osa thought, "so frightful as to be magnificent."

Osa could barely believe it, but Martin began cranking the movie camera. She smiled nervously as the chief walked toward her. Martin talked to her encouragingly, telling her to not look afraid. "I clung to the sound of his voice," Osa said, "as to the one sane thing left in a world gone grotesquely mad." She offered Nagapate tobacco, but he ignored it. She then tried a piece of red calico. He reached out, but instead of taking the fabric, he took her arm. He rubbed her skin, puzzled by the color. He scraped it with a piece of cane, thinking she must be painted, and marveled at its pink reaction. He shook his head and removed Osa's hat to reveal her blondish hair, which only puzzled him further.

With night about to fall and not knowing what the chief would do next, Martin removed the camera from its tripod and moved between Nagapate and Osa, reaching out his hand to the chief to

Nagapate stands amid the split drums (*boo-boos*) that haunted Martin and Osa's time in the South Seas.

shake good-bye. Nagapate did not like this gesture, and Martin whispered to Osa to head toward the trail. She moved, and Nagapate caught her arm. He took her hand and shook it, like Martin had just done to his. She took this as friendliness, but Nagapate had no idea of its meaning. He held on to her, further examining her cheeks and hair, and prodding her curiously. Suddenly, Nagapate dropped her arm and yelled an order to his men. Some of them went running into the forest, while the others seized Osa and Martin. Osa screamed as they dragged her toward the jungle. "Every ghastly tale I had ever heard came crowding into my memory," said Martin, "and as I looked at the ring of black, merciless faces, and saw my wife sagging, half-swooning, in the arms of her cannibal captors, my heart almost stopped its beating."

The movement and noise abruptly stopped. The natives began to whisper, and Martin took advantage of the distraction to pull away from his captors. Nagapate came back into the clearing and looked down to the bay. Martin followed his gaze and saw a British patrol boat in the water. Feigning confidence, Martin told Nagapate the war ship was there looking for them. Nagapate yelled an order to his men who then released Osa. She immediately started running for the trail. Martin called to her to slow down so as not to seem afraid. She did, but once out of sight, she sprinted.

Osa and Martin ran through the dense jungle, which tore at their clothes. Wet leaves slapped their flesh. In the darkness, they could not see the trail and fell down several drops without slowing down. It seemed to Martin they had run for hours, and they were only halfway down the mountain. They could see in the breaks of forest that the British ship was pulling away. Behind them, native drums began to beat. Osa fell into a pool of mud, and they realized they were lost. Martin took her in his arms. This brief pause gave them a moment to relocate the trail, which they had lost in their panic. Osa, who could see better in the dark than Martin, led the way. They began to hear natives shouting behind them and rushed toward the beach. The setting sun glared at them and the sand slowed down their sprint as the native voices grew closer. Though his hand was shaking, Martin reached for Osa's arm. They ran into the water, where their assistants, who had apparently escaped long ago, dragged them onto the boat. As they pulled away, the Big Nambas emerged from the jungle, shouting at them from the beach.

Despite this hair-raising adventure and the later development of fevers and sores that had him bed-ridden, Martin wrote a letter to a friend two weeks after leaving the South Seas, claiming he was having the time of his life. "[W]e both hate to leave it," he said of the region. "[I]t has sores, fevers, mosquitoes, savages, storms, and millions of bugs and insects but," he continued, "it is the most attractive place in the world." Even after their frightening episode on Malukula, Martin believed that Osa too wished to return. "Osa is just as bad as I am," he revealed, "you will see that she will be just as bad as me from now on."

———

"They risked their lives every second of their perilous trip," proclaimed advertisements for Martin and Osa's film *Cannibals of the South Seas,* "but they returned with the most remarkable authentic pictures ever filmed of the least known people on the face of the earth." Released in 1916, *Cannibals* was the couple's first film together, created with footage from this first trip. Posters featured a stern-looking Nagapate with bushy hair and beard, furrowed brow, and menacing bone through his nose. "[P]hotographed at the risk of life," read the caption.

The appeal of the film went beyond Nagapate's sinister scowl: Audiences were intrigued by the husband-and-wife team of adventurers. Due to this, advertisers at their distributer, Robertson-Cole, played up the dynamics of married adventure. Martin and his "plucky little wife," their ad proclaimed, had traveled thousands of miles to risk their lives for a film "rife with the spirit of adventure, the lure of azure seas and green savage isles, the undying romance of Conrad, Stevenson and London." Osa was young and attractive, making people wonder at her chosen lifestyle. The San Francisco *Daily News* reported: "Osa Johnson has weighed civilization in the balance and found it wanting." "No tiled kitchen and wall beds for this young matron," the article continued. "She finds civilization empty after her adventures in the South Seas. . . ."

Osa's ability to balance an adventurous lifestyle with urban sophistication was unique. "I had pictured her as reflecting some of the color of her South Sea Island existence," wrote one interviewer who met Osa in New York, "and was surprised to see standing before me a fair-haired, slender young woman who looked as if she has never been away from Broadway and its alluring atmosphere." Sitting with Osa in her New York City apartment, the reporter watched as she gently spoke to the parrots she had brought back with her from the South Seas. They seemed to recognize and acknowledge her. When asked if she had felt afraid in the islands, Osa replied, "I was frightened, of course, though I loved the free outdoor life." But, more important, Osa wanted to be at Martin's side. They had, she said, "never been separated a day" in their nine years of marriage, and "she insisted on facing all the dangers with him."

While Osa was a glamorous and intriguing celebrity, Martin's respect among Hollywood, photographers, and explorers grew. He appeared in advertisements for Peerless Standard Projection Company and Universal Motion Pictures Cameras. In May 1919, a magazine called *The Picture Show* praised his work: "Martin Johnson has shown the world that the camera is the greatest weapon of modern exploration." He was at once a camera man, a scientist, and the bravest of men. He "risks his all to get his most amazing living drama."

The footage of Nagapate fondling Osa shocked audiences. Instead of garnering understanding of indigenous cultures, it testified to the dangers of the so-called savages. When the film was released, racial tensions in the United States were at a peak. Spurred by competition for jobs and an American delegate's rejection of an international racial equality proposal, white-black riots raged throughout American cities beginning in April 1919 and continued through what was dubbed the Red Summer. American attitudes toward dark-skinned people in other nations were no better. Portrayals of them on screen often painted them as irrational and violent savages bent on killing white men and violating white women, playing upon the racial fears and tensions at home.

On screen, Osa emerged as a real-life and cinematic heroine. "She has known woman's ultimate terror . . . and matched wits and beauty against the bestial power of a black tyrant," praised one reviewer. Martin was more certain now than ever that Osa was the brave partner he needed for his work. He dedicated his book *Cannibals of the South Seas* (1919) to his mother, "who has continuously protested against my trips into out-of-the-way places," his father, "who has over-ruled the protestations of my mother because he would love to share my adventures," and to Osa, "my ideal of a woman—a help-mate in every sense of the word."

In January 1919, Martin and Osa were living in New York City, where Martin handled the growing distribution of the film. In some cities, including Chicago, censors banned or cut parts of the film, refusing to show it in its entirety. "Naturally," wrote Martin, "we could not stand for that." Addressing their issues with near nudity, Martin replied, "a few narrow brained censors would not stand for nature as it is in the many thousands of South Sea Islands." Some stockholders in Martin's work wanted out. He offered to buy their stock but told them they should wait—in just a few months they would see a profit from the film, and those from his next expedition.

As Martin prepared to return to the South Seas, Robertson-Cole hired a publicist dedicated solely to his work. Though disappointed in the lack of profits brought in by the first feature, the company supported another expedition and film. In the meantime, they cut the original film into ten single-reel films to make the most of the footage. As Osa and Martin began getting ready for their return to the South Seas, the demands of promotion overwhelmed their time. Newspapers around the nation ran articles about their upcoming adventure, and the couple was filmed everywhere they went for newsreels. They made appearances at theaters across the country and met with "practically every big moving picture star in Los Angeles." "[W]e are going to work our damnedest to outdo anything we have ever done before," Martin assured his supporters.

On April 8, 1919, Martin and Osa again sailed for the South Seas, hoping to "bring back the most wonderful pictures ever made." As they sailed, Osa wrote to her parents, telling them how much she already missed them. "Somehow I feel so depressed and lonely," she wrote, thinking about the two long years she and Martin planned to spend abroad. She revealed her hesitation toward this lifestyle, telling her parents that after this adventure, she hoped they would "stay home in this country."

Once in Sydney, Australia, however, Osa's spirits lifted. She found the people friendly and was impressed with how many wealthy Australians were interested in meeting the young American adventurers. She and Martin were invited to formal dinners nearly every night, and Osa delighted in dressing up for these occasions. Even Martin, she said, "dolls up all the time." She befriended the wife of a captain's son who had just had a baby but welcomed the chance to escape with Osa in the captain's "lovely car."

After six weeks in Sydney, Osa and Martin sailed to Port Vila, the capital of the New Hebrides, where they ran into their old friend Father Prin, who had left his mission on Vao. Once again, Martin and Osa had a difficult time getting a boat to take them to Malekula. They found a captain willing to take them to Espiritu Santo, an island two hundred miles north of Malekula, and thought that may be as close as they could get for the time being. At a supply stop along the route, Martin saw a familiar boat in port. It was the *Snark*, now filthy and used as a blackbirding ship for the slave trade. "Frowzy and unbelievably dirty," thought Osa, "she reminded me somehow of an aristocrat fallen upon evil days."

From Espiritu Santo, they easily found a ship to Vao and arranged for transportation from there to Malekula via three schooners trading in the region. Without Father Prin, however, Vao seemed to Osa "lonely and desolate." The natives stared at them when they arrived on the beach, only helping them when offered tobacco. Martin and Osa stayed in Father Prin's former home but felt constantly watched. "[E]ven if I'm not in a cage," Martin said, "I'll always know how a monkey feels." After her last experience, Osa packed more comforts for this trip, including air mattresses, a Primus stove, and bacon, ham, and cheese stored in chop boxes. These things made her feel more at ease. "I settled down to make my home," she mused, looking around Father Prin's old house, "in what is considered one of the wildest lands of the world."

Shortly after they settled in, twenty Malekulan men from the Small Nambas tribe arrived on the beach at Vao in canoes. They told Martin and Osa that they had been driven from Malekula by violent Big Nambas attacks. The tribe had taken their women and children captive and killed many of their men. The Small Nambas chief, Tethlong, led the remaining people to Vao, where they sought refuge. Tethlong established himself as chief among the Vao natives by holding a five-day feast with singing, dancing, drumming, and feasting. Martin took pictures of the festival but worried about the balance of power on the island and began anxiously awaiting the schooners that had promised to pick them up and take them to Malekula.

Meanwhile, Osa befriended one of Father Prin's converted boys and trained him to help her around the house. She planted a vegetable garden and established a regular routine, baking fresh bread every Saturday and doing the wash on Monday. She prepared large meals and sat with Martin every night for dinner. Martin set up his laboratory to develop still pictures and prints, and exposed those he took at the feast. The pair became quite at home in the tropics, speaking Beche-de-Mer to each other even when alone. "There is something fascinating about this queer, garbled English," wrote Osa. "I found myself actually thinking in this peculiar patois of the tropics."

Under Tethlong's leadership, the Vao and Malekula natives were growing friendlier, and Vao canoes shuttled refugees over every night, accompanied by eerie chants and drumming. On one particularly picturesque night, Osa was watching the full moon when she was startled by a native canoe cutting through the water. She looked on as the silent natives rowed to the beach and lifted "a long, heavy object wrapped in leaves" out of the boat. They carried the package to their village, from which the sound of drums and chanting soon arose. Suspecting this was a cannibal ritual, Martin and Osa sat in the house wide awake for the rest of the night with their guns at their sides. "The tropical night had lost its beauty," lamented Osa, "and was filled with a grisly menace."

In the morning, Martin and Osa were thrilled to see one of the trade schooners at anchor. Osa felt confident that the Malekulan natives would not try to harm them this time while so many traders and sailors were ashore. The Johnsons took this opportunity to paddle to Malekula with the owner of the schooners, Paul Mazouyer. They were met on the beach by twenty Big Nambas, including Nagapate. "Oddly enough," Osa said, "Nagapate was now a screen personality to me rather than a savage, and somehow I had lost my terror of him." Martin felt the same, and with a courage born from familiarity, they went straight toward him to shake his hand. "The cannibal chief seemed puzzled at first," said Osa, "but he could see we held no grudge for his apparent culinary intentions on our first visit, and became almost genial."

The trust and friendliness went both ways. Nagapate asked to go on board a schooner, something most natives were reluctant to do because of the fear of being blackbirded. On board, Osa fed him and his two companions while Martin took their photographs. Then they showed Nagapate photos of himself from their last trip. "[H]e started incredulously," Osa noticed, "showed it to his two men, then all three let out blood-curdling yells." They stood amazed in front of a life-size poster of Nagapate promoting *Cannibals of the South Seas,* taking turns touching it and backing away in awe. This peaceful meeting made Osa and Martin ecstatic. They had feared Nagapate would still be unwelcoming. Now, Martin knew he would have a chance to film the lives of the Big Nambas people. "We had brought armed men, and here, on the deck of our schooner within three feet of us, blinking and content sat Nagapate," enthused Osa, "with no more violence in him apparently than might be found in an old fat toad."

Martin brought Osa her ukulele and, with a kiss on the cheek, told her to play for the visiting chief. Her music made Nagapate grunt and mumble to his men. When she sang the Hawaiian song "Aloha," however, the men tilted their heads side to side rhythmically and began to chant in time, as if the tune were familiar. Osa noticed Nagapate's "face was alight, his eyes closed and he swayed from side to side." When he grew aware of this, he scowled and

For their screening on Malekula, Martin hung oversized posters announcing the film *Cannibals of the South Seas.*

motioned to leave. He was embarrassed at having let his guard down. The next day his men brought yams, coconuts, and fruits to the boat and laid them at Osa's feet, an offering of peace. The natives did not treat their own women as leaders, and Mazouyer, who was familiar with their ways, was astounded at this offering to a female. Mazouyer and Martin joked that Nagapate must have thought Osa "the boss of the expedition."

Martin and Osa returned to the beach, laid down trade goods, and set up their cameras. This attracted the attention of a good number of Big Nambas men. Many came to the beach, but Nagapate was among the last to arrive. Late in the afternoon, Martin began to set up a screen and projector. He made sure Mazouyer and the other men watched the Nambas closely as he was unsure how they would react to these new technologies. Meanwhile, Osa diverted their attention with ukelele songs. Martin was still fiddling with his equipment. He could not get the generator working to power the projector. As night began to fall, the men started to leave. He and Osa pleaded with them to stay, but the men did not understand why they should remain. Finally, the generator started up, illuminating the screen with a single stream of light from the projector. The Nambas eyed the beam from the projector suspiciously. Osa took Nagapate by the arm and sat on the ground facing the screen, waiting for the film to begin. "Clearly he didn't like being pushed around by a woman," thought Osa, "but he sat down beside me, apparently to think it over."

Then the film began. The natives looked at the screen titles and the beam of light over their heads, "chattering like mad." The first image on screen was of Osa. "They were literally struck dumb," said Osa. "Here I was on the beach sitting beside Nagapate—and there I was on the screen as big as a giant. Then the picture of me winked at them. This threw them into a furor. They shrieked with laughter. They howled and screamed." The film then showed Osa and Martin leaving the Waldorf Astoria Hotel and walking through the crowded streets of Manhattan. When Nagapate looked troubled, Osa surmised it was because he had not realized there were so many white people in the world. They must have, he indicated to Osa, a very large island to live on.

Martin had set up his moving picture camera on the beach to capture the natives' reactions to *Cannibals of the South Seas*. When Nagapate's face appeared on the screen, "a great roar went up" and his people yelled his name. But it was too dark for Martin to get the right exposure, so he set off radium flares to illuminate the scene, sending some of the Big Nambas scattering into the forest. Osa looked at Nagapate reassuringly. "This sort of business," Osa tried to convey to him, "was an every day occurrence in the lives of white people." As the film progressed, many of the natives who had stayed behind began to recognize themselves on screen and call each others' names as they appeared, laughing. When a man who had since died appeared, they fell silent. "The natives were awe-struck," indicated Osa. "Martin's 'magic' had brought a dead man from his grave." When the film ended, the people milled about, expecting tobacco as payment for watching the film. Osa handed it out, and they packed their equipment. As they were about to leave, a messenger came with an invitation from Nagapate to come into the village. Remembering their last visit to the village, the messenger promised, "He no makem bad, he makem good altogether."

The next morning, they walked up the trail to Nagapate's village with their thirty-one companions. Osa's first encounter with Nagapate may have made her famous, but it was not a thing she wished to repeat, and she took comfort in the fact that a number of their party were armed. They hiked till noon, then rested in a clearing where Nagapate's men met them and helped carry their equipment to the village. When they arrived, Nagapate entered the center circle of the village accompanied by drumming. He drank from a bamboo water bottle, which he passed around for them to drink from, beginning with Osa. After Martin gave gifts to Nagapate and tobacco to his men, he took pictures of the people. Osa coaxed a man to demonstrate going in and out of the low entrance of a hut on his hands and knees. The other men made fun of him, and the Johnsons had a difficult time getting action shots after that.

Just as they were beginning to wonder where the Big Nambas hid their women, they saw a few looking out at them from the forest. Wishing to coax them into better light, Osa approached the women, but they ran to hide. As she watched them cower with fright, she felt sorry for their pitiful state. "I'm sure that no human creatures were ever so wretched as these poor daughters of Eve," she wrote. Because of a taboo on female bathing, the women were filthy. They wore heavy, dirt-encrusted grass skirts that fell to their knees and veils of grass that cascaded to the ground. "It was heavy, cumbersome and unsanitary, and, as they moved about, it gave them the look," said Osa, "of animated hay stacks."

Martin and Osa stayed for several days in the village but struggled to get action shots. One of the tribe's leaders seemed to understand the camera and played the clown in front of it, which they encouraged, hoping others would do the same. Meanwhile, Martin and Osa explored the forest. Along one of the trails, they found a large hut with a basket of shrunken human heads sitting inside. "More grinned at us from the eaves," cringed Osa. Bones were piled in all four corners. Knowing this must be some kind of ceremonial or sacred place, they quickly exited the hut, hoping no one had seen them. Regrettably, Martin did not go back to the hut to take pictures. "The best pictures," he indicated remorsefully, "like the biggest fish, are the ones you don't get."

After six days in the village, the natives grew bored with the Johnsons and their cameras. Of more concern, however, was Nagapate's affection for Osa. He brought her gifts every morning and followed her around the village all day long. Mazouyer and Martin agreed they should leave before something went wrong. Nagapate escorted them to the beach the following morning and came on board the schooner for a meal. He asked to sleep on the ship, so they set up beds for him and his men in the engine room. This trust, Osa thought, was "the greatest compliment, certainly, that the savage chief could have paid us." Martin and Osa found it difficult to completely adjust their views of these people, whose violent nature was legendary but who had caused them no harm.

The schooner returned Martin and Osa to Vao, where Martin worked developing the plates and moving-pictures films he had taken on Malekula. After looking at his work, he told Osa he wanted to sail all the way around Malekula, land in each port, and photograph its residents. She was disappointed at the delay in heading home. They had spent seven months "among dirt-encrusted man-eating strangers," and Osa realized she was ready for her "own people." "Every now and then I wanted 'home' so terribly," she said, "I even found myself longing for a nice tall foamy ice cream soda."

While they waited for their chance to return to Malekula, Martin and Osa explored Vao and took pictures of its people. Martin was not intrigued by them, however. He thought them rather too tame after experiencing life among the Big Nambas. They also found they had more trouble communicating with these people now than they had just a few years ago. The younger people used words they had never heard in Beche-de-Mer and mingled it with French and English in "strange corruptions." Beyond language, Martin and Osa wondered at the people's customs, especially the hard labor of the tribe's women. They were in charge of paddling canoes to collect firewood from Malekula. A man accompanied each canoe, but only as an armed guard, and did not assist the women in their tasks.

They observed feasts that the people held for births, deaths, and upon the completion of houses, canoes, and *devil-devils* (totems). One feast for a devil-devil began with the presentation of the object, then a massive meal of one hundred pigs and chickens—all killed and cooked on the spot. The elders prepared the fires and distributed food, but also received some as gifts, in a communal potluck. The chief cooked for himself. After eating, the people danced in what seemed to be imitations of the pig and chicken sacrifices just performed. Soon they broke into other dances, and Martin reflected, "I never saw a native do exactly the same dance twice. . . ." Martin and Osa left the ceremony, but from the house they could hear the boo-boos drone on until dawn.

Though they made the most of their time on Vao, Martin and Osa were neither filming the isolated tribes of Malekula nor getting any closer to the home for which Osa longed. To make things worse, they witnessed several unusual rituals that increased Osa's desire to leave the island. While walking down the beach one day, she saw an old man living alone in a hut who looked as if he were starving. She sent her native friend with food. The following day, they found the man buried, presumably alive. The people explained nonchalantly that he had lived long enough, and live burial was how they dealt with the matter. Osa's gift had drawn attention to the man, who was trying to remain alive a little longer.

On another day, Martin and Osa were in the house when they heard a piercing scream from the village. They ran to see what had happened and found a woman lying on the ground. She had holes burnt in the backs of her knees and was in excruciating pain. Osa "turned away, half sick." This was, they learned, the punishment for a woman who tried to run away from her husband. She was the wife of chief Nowdi, who had paid twenty pigs for her and was angered that she kept trying to leave him. As retaliation, he pressed scalding stones into the backs of her knees to cripple her. "It was hard for me to keep my hands off the brutes that stood laughing around the girl," fumed Martin. "Only the knowledge that to touch them would be suicide for me and death or worse for Osa held me back." His passions roused, Martin tried to rationalize the situation by telling himself he should not judge other cultures "still in the stage of development passed by our own ancestors hundreds of thousands of years ago."

That non-Western cultures were in an early stage of development was a common theory at the time. It was actually meant to foster understanding and create a common bond between cultures, but often it only led people to look down upon more "primitive" or "savage" peoples and attempt to "civilize" them. Martin and Osa, however, respected the differences, even as they found them repulsive. The standards of "civilized society," Martin explained, were quite different, and not all were good. Even those from so-called civilized societies sometimes grew "beastly" when "released from the restraints of civilization."

After a full month on Vao, another boat, the *Amour,* anchored offshore. Martin and Osa paddled out to find an old acquaintance, Capt. Charles Moran, and his brother, an engineer. Both were born in the South Seas and knew the islands and their people well. They were sailing around collecting copra (coconuts) but agreed to take the Johnsons around Malekula for photographs. Three days into their journey, they stopped at Lambuma (Lumbumba) Bay, which connects the northern and southern portions of the island. Seldom-seen nomadic tribes were rumored to reside here. They were so infrequently seen, many thought them a myth. This mystery made Martin determined to photograph them if he could, so they scouted the area. On the first day they saw nothing, but on the morning of the second day, they discovered baskets and the warm embers of recent fires. Shortly after that find, Martin literally bumped right into a native without even seeing him. The man ran directly into the jungle and out of sight.

Martin tried to content himself with taking pictures of impressive banyan trees until the native people returned. When he noticed four men looking at him from behind the branches of a banyan, he offered them the usual gifts of tobacco, salt, and calico. The people were unfamiliar with these common South Seas trade goods and showed no interest in them at all. After an hour of frustrated attempts to get the men to come onto the beach, Martin organized the ship's crew to help force them out into better lighting. But when they returned to the spot, the natives had disappeared.

The next morning, a man came to the beach and, speaking Beche-de-Mer, asked the Johnsons what they wanted. Martin and Osa were astonished. They had not expected such easy communication from one of these elusive nomads. The man explained that he had been blackbirded and lived away from the tribe for years before making his way back. The Johnsons offered him tobacco, a pipe, and matches in exchange for guiding them into the forest to meet the other people of his tribe. The people had thick black hair and an odd separation between their big toe and the other smaller toes. Five of the tribe approached and examined the Johnsons, touching their boots and marveling at Osa's blonde hair. "I felt no apprehension whatever," said Osa, "[their] appearance, while grotesque, was peaceful."

Twenty more natives came forward, and Osa snapped still photographs while Martin cranked the moving-picture camera. The noise disturbed the people, who ran and jumped up into a banyan tree. Watching them grasp the vines with their feet, Martin realized why their toes were so strangely separated. It was from climbing trees. The chief, Wo-bang-an-ar, was friendly and allowed Martin to photograph him all afternoon. The next day, their guide took them farther into the forest to a village of one hundred people. There were no houses, and it seemed that the people lived in the trees. They wore the same pandanus fiber as the Nambas, had bows and arrows, and somehow had acquired guns. Martin and Osa saw no signs of cannibalism among these people, with whom they stayed for several days.

Back aboard the *Amour*, they anchored off the southwestern coast of Malekula late at night. In the morning, they paddled to a lagoon filled with small islands and a "lovely scene," even if marred by the "fetid smell of rotting vegetation." Natives approached them in canoes, indicating they should follow them to land. These people had long heads, shaped by boards in infancy. Their villages had only three or four ramshackle huts and decaying devil-devils. This decreptitude, like the nomadic state of the people they met earlier, was the result of island warfare. Inside the huts, signs of cannibalism hung from the rafters—human heads and curious mummified bodies. Still, the people did not instill any fear in the Johnsons, who felt somewhat sorry for their state of seemingly hopeless decay.

The Johnsons sailed farther down the coast, where the forest began to dangle directly into the water, creating idyllic scenery but no places in which they could reach land. At last they came upon a beach on which they noticed baskets hanging from trees. As they began to pull ashore, twenty armed natives painted "in dizzying designs" of white, red, yellow, and blue emerged from the forest. They had feathers stuck into their hair, and they seemed to Osa the scariest of the people they had seen so far. Neither Martin nor the captain could get the crew to pull into shore. Anxious to meet these men, Martin plunged into the water and swam to the beach. He held out tobacco and indicated they could have it if they laid down their guns. The people went into the forest and came back out unarmed. They seemed impressed with Martin's boldness.

The men invited Martin to a ceremony. He returned to the boat to fetch his cameras and Osa, then allowed the natives to guide them through the forest. Osa did her best to ignore the ominous sound of beating boo-boos, which she admitted sent "chill[s] down my spine." They climbed to the top of a hill and found a clearing filled with large boo-boos and devil-devils, and what seemed like a thousand natives. The drumming stopped as they approached the "fiercest-looking" people they had ever set eyes upon. An elder approached them, and Martin presented gifts to all the chiefs. As he set up his camera, the natives ran away. One old chief, colored with yellow ocher, remained. He examined the camera while Martin attempted to explain its purpose. The chief signaled for the people to come back, but he did not look entirely pleased. Men, women, and children resumed their ceremony with dancing, leaping, and yelling as they moved around in a circle. Several groups took turns doing different dances. "It was a wonderful sight," said Martin. "My 'movie' sense completely overcame my fears, and I ground out roll after roll of film."

When the sun began to set, Captain Moran and Osa urged him to stop filming so they could leave, but Martin just lit flares and kept cranking his camera. As the dance progressed, it seemed to be getting faster, more frantic. Her fear growing, Osa pleaded with Martin to leave. He acquiesced and, as they were about to take off, laid down tobacco as thanks to the natives. The well-intentioned offering caused a stir among the people. Osa ran immediately, fearing for their lives. Moran and Martin tried not to show their fear and backed slowly toward the trail as the natives fought over the tobacco. When the men caught up with Osa, she was crying with rage and scolded Martin for putting them in such danger. "I took the scolding . . . , for I knew she was right," said Martin, though he wished he could have stayed until the end of the dance for the sake of the film.

Moran told the Johnsons of a tribe he knew that still smoked human heads to preserve them. He traded there frequently and assured Osa it was safe. When they arrived, they found an old man in the center of the village dancing alone. Beyond him, there was a smoldering fire surrounded by several sticks, the top of each holding a human head. Martin took photographs of the smoking heads and talked to the head curer, who spoke Beche-de-Mer. The curer described the process of "seasoning" a human head: First, it was soaked in fermented herbs to harden and make it fireproof; then it was turned in the smoke, as he was currently doing, to render the fat and dry the tissue; and then smeared with clay and baked. All of this took several weeks. The people only dried the heads of dead relatives in this manner, which they then hung from the rafters inside a sacred hut, or "headhouse." Enemy heads were not given such extensive care.

Martin and Osa parted ways with Captain Moran at Port Sandwich, having fulfilled their goal of encircling Malekula. They then boarded the *Euphrosyne* guided by Commissioner King and made their way back to Vao. King first took them to Api, where they were invited to stay as guests on a large coconut plantation managed by an eccentric Englishman who dressed formally for dinner every night even in these tropical wilds. He told his guests that he wore white tie and tails even when he dined alone.

When they reached Vao, Martin and Osa were greeted by natives who were glad to see them—not because they missed them, but because they missed their tobacco. Osa was astonished that they didn't simply break into the house and take their supply. Though the native people had their vices, she reflected, stealing was not one of them. Once back in Father Prin's house, Martin began sealing the film and developing still pictures while Osa packed their bags. They began to dream of home.

Everything was nearly packed when a boat pulled up to Vao, a man named Powler at the helm. He had heard of Martin's project and had come of his own accord to offer his assistance. He

This old man explained head curing procedures and demonstrated for the Johnsons' camera.

had particularly good relationships with several native groups and knew many of their languages. This was an opportunity too good to miss—a willing and knowledgeable captain with a sturdy ship. Home would have to wait.

Martin and Osa boarded the boat, and Powler took them to the island of Espiritu Santo. In one village, unusually small men told Martin their chief was insane and every so often went on a senseless rampage, killing people without cause. They said they lived in "constant terror" and asked if these newcomers would help hang the chief. Reluctant to interfere in native affairs, Martin turned them down. In another village, people danced around devil-devils in what seemed an ordinary ceremony, but Osa had a gut feeling this was something more sinister. After a while, Powler examined the meat roasting over the fire; it was not pig. He smiled and whispered to Martin that this was his long-sought cannibal feast. Osa felt the "blood drain from [her] face" and looked away in disgust. Martin, on the other hand, was delighted. It was nighttime, and he had no choice but to set off a flare so he could take pictures. He got some exposures before the people ran away, grabbing the human meat as they did so. With the ceremony abandoned, Martin took pictures of what remained—a human head in the embers. He wrapped the head in a cloth and took it with him. Finally, he had proof—physical and photographic—that cannibal rituals still existed in the South Seas.

"I don't know when I've ever been so happy at the thought of going home," reflected Osa shortly after witnessing the cannibal feast. They had spent eight months in the South Seas, and she longed "for dear, familiar things—for my own people most of all, and for the places where I had spent my simple and uncomplicated girlhood." Martin, she said, "wanted home and his people and civilized living every bit as much as I did."

When they were back in Kansas, visiting their parents and feeling the warmth of familiar surroundings, however, even Osa felt the tug of adventure. Martin had promised he would buy Osa a house in which to make a home, but it seems her dreams had changed. Though she admitted she "was really very tired of savages," she could not imagine living a settled, ordinary life with Martin. Thus when he asked her if she would like to buy a house, she asked him where he ever got such a crazy idea.

After a few months their longing for home was sated, and they found themselves in East Malaysia, in the city of Sandakan (then the capital of British North Borneo), wound "in a spell of sheer delight." The variety of people—Chinese, Japanese, Filipino, Malays, Europeans—all with their distinctive styles of dress and behavior, fascinated Osa. Women dressed in bright silks, kimonos, sarongs, and mantillas stood out against those in more familiar European dress. Chinese lanterns hung along the streets at night. Bright, high-pitched music was a welcome contrast to the drones of island boo-boos. "Even the colors and smells were in a higher key," mused Osa after she and Martin walked through the city's streets, watching local life come alive. Martin wished he could capture the night scenes of the city, but he knew the darkness would never let him get a shot.

After a short stay in a bad hotel, Martin and Osa rented a missionary's home on a hill outside the city. It consisted of two tall, grass-roofed wooden houses that were comfortable, despite insects and lizards that tested Osa's patience. Martin was so focused on work, he did not even notice the pests. Osa tried to make a home of the rustic structures. She cleaned and organized the house, chased pests from its corners, and shot snakes invading the garden. At night, the mosquitoes were so bad they had to douse themselves with kerosene oil to keep them at bay.

In Sandakan, Martin and Osa met Sir West Ridgeway, president of the British North Borneo Company. Osa described him as "a tall, erect, keen-eyed old gentleman of seventy-five who appeared less than sixty." Ridgeway strongly discouraged Osa from the "hardships" of Borneo, which he listed as "poisonous insects, fevers, snakes, animals—and savages . . . as vicious as any on earth." "[D]eath in a hundred forms," he told them, "awaits any white man who ventures into the interior." And women—well, they ought to stay home with their mothers, Ridgeway asserted.

Martin defended Osa to Ridgeway. "I know that's how Osa looks, Sir West, soft and weak," Martin began, asking him to consider all she had done on their previous expedition. Martin continued, "There's more to her than you'd first imagine." Though Ridgeway refused to personally "sanction" her going on the expedition, he did all he could to ensure their safety, giving them a government boat, police escort, an interpreter, and four "coolie carriers"—all expenses paid.

Within the week, the intrepid young adventurers were on their way into the heart of Borneo. The boat traveled up a river lined with thatched huts and "alive with crocodiles." The landscape soon morphed into a dense and tangled jungle. Martin was delighted to find thousands of monkeys. He tested his filming equipment but found the animals were camouflaged by their dark

Osa sits in the cramped quarters of a *gobong* along Borneo's Kinabatangan River.

surroundings. "Monkeys the color of mud remained on the dark earth at the foot of the nipa-palms," said Martin, "monkeys the color of rust remained among leaves of a reddish hue, and leaping about in the high branches were gray monkeys that looked like mandrills, bug-nosed monkeys with long snouts, little black monkeys that were all tail, and brown monkeys with no tails whatever—all blending exasperatingly with the grays, greens, browns and reds of their background, or else losing themselves in the thick shadows." The light and camouflage in the tropical forest were challenges to Martin's photographic skills.

When they came across a forest with a bit more light, they tried filming again. Both Osa and Martin were excited at the newness of filming wild animals. Their agent had told them the public was becoming more interested in animals than in native peoples, encouraging them to switch their focus. Martin made some good photos of water buffaloes. When the buffaloes noticed them and charged, Martin threw Osa behind him and kept filming. She thought not of their lives being in danger, but of the camera being toppled and broken. One scream from Osa scared the animals off, but they returned to Sandakan with their first good animal films.

For a while the Johnsons based themselves in Sandakan and took off on short "experimental trips" while they planned a larger expedition up the Kinabatangan River—North Borneo's largest. They planned to follow the river 140 miles to the government station of Lamang, where a man named Holmes was commissioner. He accompanied them on some of their shorter trips and gave them advice, boatmen, and provisions for their expedition. He and Osa bonded by shooting crocodiles—a task that Osa took quite seriously after learning they devour children. Martin stuck to photographing them.

They stayed in Lamang for two days, then began their trip farther upriver in native canoes known as *gobongs*. Their expedition had eleven gobongs, enough to carry all their supplies and assistants. Their paddlers from Lamang, however, would not go the whole journey, as they preferred not to travel so far from home, so the Johnsons had to find new paddlers several times in villages along the way. Martin and Osa, with their cameras, rode in Holmes's own "de luxe gobong"—a thirty-five-foot-long, fully enclosed canoe with eight paddlers. The first canoe was filled with police who kept their guns handy, watching the shores for *hafees*—Malay pirates known to hide out where brooks entered the river.

Their first stop was Pandassan, the native capital and home to the head chief, Hadji Mohammed Nur. The chief invited the party to dinner and offered to accompany them on their expedition, summoning an entire crew simply by banging a brass gong. The chief was an asset to the expedition; the natives they met along the river were likely friendlier with Hadji along, offering them lemons, guavas, and bananas in exchange for salt. As they rode farther inland, the heat grew more intense. The jungle grew thicker and the river narrowed, bringing the forest closer around them. "My head ached," revealed Osa. "I ached all over, I was a mass of mosquito bites, and the pain in my back from the crouching position I was forced to maintain in the canoe under the low nipa-canopy, was excruciating." She tried to sleep during the day. Martin's height must have made the cramped canoe even worse for him, but Osa "never heard him complain." Still, she spoke to Holmes about pausing in a village and asking the people to build a boat that better fit their needs. At the village of Sungei Iyau, Hadji helped her communicate what she wanted, and the people agreed to have the houseboat ready upon the Johnsons' return.

"Nature seems full of strange tricks in this fantastic country, tricks designed to make miserable anyone entering it," Osa complained, describing the *nanti-dulu* ("wait-a-minute") bush, whose thorns seemed to reach out and trap her by snagging her clothing. "In some instances, however," she admitted, "nature is kind." Water-vine stems, they discovered, were filled with refreshing drinking water—nearly a pint in each.

They had traveled 250 miles from Sandakan, and Martin still struggled to photograph wildlife in the dark, dense jungle. They tried to thin the vegetation in areas to let in enough light for photography, but their disturbance of the forest scared the animals away. Hadji said they would soon reach thinner forests that might work better for Martin's cameras. As they continued to the headwaters, they picked up a baby female gibbon ape, which Osa named Kalowatt. The ape had been chained outside a hut and was quite a "pathetic little ball of silver fluff." The woman who owned the ape was slow to part with it, but she took their money in exchange for the animal. "It seemed cruel to take Kalowatt away from her, and yet crueler not to," thought Osa, "for from the looks of the frail little creature she could not have lived long without better care...." Osa put the ape in a box. Under Osa's care, Kalowatt seemed healthier every day and was soon Osa's constant companion and surrogate child.

At Penangah, the people seemed to have only the barest of contact with the outside world. They had never seen a white

Kalowatt, perched atop a motion picture camera, was among Osa's first jungle pets.

woman, though some said they had seen white men. They were, Osa thought, attractive people with lean physiques, straight hair, and Chinese facial features. Martin took pictures of the people, and then they left. Back on the river, they went through a rough stretch of rapids. "I doubt that any but the native boys could have got us with all our equipment safely over them," Osa remarked.

When they arrived at a Tenggara village, Hadji said they must stay and let the people properly play host to their chief. The Tenggara, who served the expedition sago spirits and a large feast, were curious, and they touched Osa's skin, hair, and clothes, "but wholly without offensiveness." The men wore G-strings made of tree bark, the women had fashioned skirts from the same material, and the children ran around stark naked. They had filed their teeth to points—or entirely off—and their lips and teeth were stained from chewing betel nut. Martin excitedly photographed these interesting figures and began to forget his disappointment over the animal pictures. With Hadji's help, the people happily performed for them, letting Martin film their methods of weaving, cooking, child rearing, hygiene, fire making, and even how they shot their blowguns. Osa found the women, though they worked harder than the men, "were spirited and independent and would tolerate no abuse either of themselves or their children."

The Tenggara were headhunters, as evident by human scalps dangling from their knife handles. That they continued this practice, however, was meant to be a secret since British government regulations forbade it. During the feast, Osa grew uncomfortable at the rowdiness of the drunken natives. She worried that if she rejected their offering of monkey meat, they would not take it well, and she knew she could not stomach eating monkeys. "[I]t savored too much of cannibalism," she thought. At her urging, Martin packed up his cameras, and they walked back down to the beach. When the natives saw them loading into the gobongs, they protested but were too drunk to catch up with the departing visitors.

Just one mile down river, Martin and Osa found the thinner forest Hadji had promised, and they stopped, walking into the jungle in the hopes of securing pictures of Borneo's fascinating monkeys and apes. In the night, they were awoken by sounds of screaming, which their guides told them was an orangutan. The strange noises continued through the night, and, in the morning, they found the orangutan perched in a tree just above their camp. "I don't think I've ever seen Martin more excited," said Osa, "not even when he got his camera ready for his first picture of Nagapate." The men tried to scare the ape into the open, but it leaped along the treetops, making it hard for Martin to photograph it.

He followed with his camera, and Osa saw that hopeful "glint in his eye." Martin, Osa, and their guides chased the ape all day. "I could have sworn that at times he actually laughed at us," remarked Osa.

At the end of the day, however, they had no decent pictures of the animal. Osa was so tired of trudging through the jungle that she swore if she were snagged by another nanti-dulu bush or had to pull another leech off her body, she'd "start screaming and nothing could stop me." Weary and frustrated, Osa and Martin called it a day. They began working their way back to camp but found they could not orient themselves. The orangutan had led them on such a mazelike chase that even the guides were confused. After several failed attempts by the guides to get back, Osa felt she was about to break down and cry. Though she tried to hide her tears from Martin, he put his arm around her and said he'd take over. She noticed his dirty-blond hair was so soaked through with humidity and sweat that his curls stuck to his forehead. "He was anxious and earnest and disappointed over everything and just as tired as I was," remarked Osa. "I had found that there is nothing quite so heartening to a man as knowing his woman has confidence in him," so she followed the path he thought would take them to camp. But in truth, he did not know his way any better than the guides did. "We might as well have been at the bottom of a deep green ocean," Osa lamented. In the end, Martin's instincts proved right. Under his leadership, they found their way to camp in under an hour.

Martin was disheartened. He could not figure out the tricks of jungle photography. In fact, no one had. Without proper lighting, shooting in such dark, natural environments was impossible for the technology of the day. What's more, the animals did not cooperate. What was not already camouflaged, ran and hid in the dense vegetation. His spirits were lifted, however, when they returned to Sungei Iyau and saw the houseboat Osa had commissioned. Surprised and pleased, Martin gave Osa a hug and immediately tested the bed. Osa and Martin both put on clean clothes and tidied up for dinner, inviting Holmes and Hadji to dine on their houseboat with them. Osa prepared what comfort food she could from their remaining mixture of canned and wild goods, and they dined on biscuits, tea, shrimp, clams, game birds, mushrooms, spinach, yams, rice, and a dessert of wild fruits. Kalowatt roamed freely and playfully around the boat, which felt more like home than anything they had seen so far in Borneo.

"I believe that Martin's love extended to practically every creature that lived," mused Osa, wondering at his desire to keep two hairy spiders as pets. While Osa enjoyed pets, the spiders were not her idea of cuddly creatures. At a rubber plantation they acquired a female orangutan whom they named Bessie, who proved to be a perfect playmate for Kalowatt. Though Osa tolerated the spiders, she drew the line when Martin brought a basket of cobras on board. Kalowatt and Bessie, who screeched at the reptiles, also objected.

Oddly, animals seemed easier to collect than photographs. Back in Pandassan, natives brought a captive honey bear, native deer, and several monkeys to Martin to photograph. They seemed to understand, if vaguely, that Martin needed animals from the forest. This was not, however, how Martin wished to film wildlife. He took some pictures of these captives, then let them loose in the forest, hoping to find wildlife in its natural habitat before they had to leave Borneo. He felt a glimmer of hope when he heard rumors of elephants near Lamang, but when they went to find them, they could not. "The jungle continued to present its green, solid, inscrutable face," groused Osa.

Disappointed, they headed back to Sandakan, where they lamented their journey. Martin felt that the trip had been a waste of money; he should have known the difficulties and been more prepared. Despite this, Martin was determined to find elephants before leaving Borneo, so they took the government boat twenty miles up one last river to known elephant country, accompanied by four hunters and six assistants. From the river they hiked through the jungle for three days contemplating "the abundant and sometimes repellent beauties of the Borneo jungle." "Trees of strange shapes sometimes tied themselves in complete knots in their efforts to reach the light," observed Osa. "[S]ome bore leaves of deep red and lemon yellow that gave the effect of sunlight where there was none." After months of exploring, they were still uncovering the tricks of the landscape. They thought sleeping in banyan trees the safest option but were swarmed by mosquitoes. "Why in the world did we ever pick Borneo," asked Osa, as she worried about snakes crawling along the jungle floor. "Oh, I charged that up to just plain dumbness on my part long ago," replied Martin with a laugh.

Early that morning, they found their men had already started through the forest to try to scare an elephant herd closer to camp. Martin set up his camera and told Osa to climb a tree and have her gun ready. He began cranking the moving-picture camera as the herd approached, and he filmed until they were within thirty-five feet of where he stood. Then, excited, he speedily grabbed the camera and climbed the tree, filming from above. He threw his pith helmet into the middle of the herd, hoping they'd trample it so he could bring back "a fine souvenir" of the thrilling adventure. After Martin was content he had gotten enough pictures, the men attempted to drive the elephants off; however, the animals momentarily turned on the men. Martin continued to crank his camera. Once the men had finally scared the elephants off, Martin and Osa climbed down the tree, relieved they had all escaped unscathed.

On their way back to Sandakan, they came across another herd of elephants, bathing in the river. They drifted slowly in their gobong, taking pictures until the animals noticed them and took cover in the forest. No longer feeling as if they'd thrown their hard-earned money away, Martin and Osa decided to head home. And they were right—the elephant photos saved the expedition.

Sir West Ridgeway bid them a warm farewell as they boarded a freighter for Singapore with Kalowatt, Bessie, and a collection of cockatoos. The freighter was crawling with roaches, served "unnameable" food, and had "other discomforts too numerous to mention," said Osa. "[B]ut I minded them very little," she continued. "Apparently I was becoming a hardened traveler like Martin; like Charmian London. Perhaps, I reflected hopefully, I had even taken on the look of one."

CHAPTER 3

TAKING AIM AT AFRICA

To me, Africa will always mean the wilderness.

—MARTIN JOHNSON

It was no sooner dark than all about us lions began roaring. Somehow it had never occurred to me that there would be so many in one place, not even in Africa. I hoped I didn't look as nervous as I felt...

—OSA JOHNSON

In 1921 Martin was inducted into the most prestigious club of its kind—the Explorers Club. He joined the ranks of such famous adventurers as Theodore Roosevelt, Sir Ernest Shackleton, Robert Peary, and Knud Rasmussen. On his application for admission, Martin cited his "Around the World" education. Women, however, were not yet allowed membership in the Explorers Club, so Osa was not even considered, despite braving the very same perils as her husband. When fellow member and biologist

Carl Akeley saw the Johnsons' photos, he encouraged them to take their cameras to Africa. "You have a very important mission, Martin," he confided. "Even more important than mine . . . I've made it my mission to perpetuate vanishing wild-animal life in bronze and by securing specimens for the museum. You are doing the same thing in film, which is available to millions of people all over the world."

Later that year, Martin, Osa, the gibbon ape Kalowatt, and Martin's father, John, sailed from New York City for the fabled Dark Continent (they had left Bessie in the care of the Central Park Zoo). John was seventy years old, a widower, and had just sold his jewelry store so he could "set out to see the world," as he put it, with his adventuring son. When they landed at Mombasa, their eighty-five trunks of supplies took three days to get through customs. Once through, they immediately reloaded the trunks onto a train for Nairobi.

Initially, Osa found the African climate extremely hot and humid. John said it was "no worse than summers in Kansas" and helped Martin with the trunks and equipment check—tasks Osa had done in the South Seas. "The boss of an outfit," he told her so she wouldn't feel useless, "never works. . . . You sit there." So she sat in the shade watching the men sort through their supplies. If there was no shade, John hired a native to hold an umbrella over her.

When everything was repacked, the Johnson party rode out of Mombasa in a train car bound for Nairobi. Though modern, the train cars were not as luxurious as American Pullman sleeping cars, to which they were accustomed from their vaudeville days. However, Osa had packed their own bedding and pillows, which made the ride quite comfortable. The train cut through groves of exotic fruits—coconuts, mangoes, papayas, and bananas—where monkeys swung and chattered from the trees. It stopped at many small stations where locals sold gourds filled with milk and what Osa thought was an unappetizing assortment of greasy-looking food to the third- and fourth-class passengers.

Though the landscape was exotic and interesting, it was not the Africa any of them had imagined. "We were eager to get to the wilds of Africa," they agreed, "but here, on all sides, we saw evidence of the hand of man." So Martin, Osa, and John went to sleep early, anxious to awake in wilder country. "No matter how much you travel, the anticipation of the unknown never grows less," mused Martin as the train sped through the countryside. "I have been five times around the world and have spent the greater part of the last twenty years in strange lands, and yet I find myself eager as a boy for each new adventure."

In the morning, Martin was the first to awake. He found Kalowatt whimpering at the window. Passing on the outside was a clearing made to build the railway, but just beyond its edge were the low-lying trees of a semi-tropical forest. On the border between clearing and forest, Martin made out "the shapes of animals, vague in the misty light." He could not identify them— "They were just mysterious forms, some horned, some hornless, some tiny and quick in movement, some as large and heavy as oxen." He found the lack of fences, embankments, and telegraph poles "added an unreality to the scene." "The train," he continued, "seemed simply to be wandering at will through the forest."

Soon John awoke and watched the scenery unfold with Martin. Osa was the last to rise, finding the "wild bush" had replaced the tropical fruit plantations of the previous day. All day long they watched wildlife in the distance. Every moment was filled with glimpses of game that, as the sun shifted, became more than mere silhouettes. Still, their newness to African wildlife and sunlight kept them from confidently identifying them. "I didn't know there were so many animals in the world," John marveled.

The scenery was broken only by the train's frequent stops. The Johnsons ate breakfast at the town of Voi, where the station dining hall reminded them of the Harvey restaurants on the Old Santa Fe Railroad in the States. Though the restaurant was forged of galvanized iron instead of wood, the servers announced meals by the same din of a gong. It reminded the Johnsons of traveling through their own Southwest. The houses of Voi's inhabitants—constructed of flattened gasoline cans and topped with grass roofs—were less familiar, however. As American Indians did outside the Harvey houses, natives here greeted each train as it arrived at the station, selling an assortment of goods and offering services as guides and translators. They were "the blackest of black African negroes," the Johnsons agreed, and though they were mostly naked, Osa thought their chosen adornments of animal skins and jewelry were "fantastic."

As the train traveled on from Voi, the Johnsons watched rolling plains reminiscent of the Kansan landscape. "It is curious how, in foreign lands, one is always being reminded of home," they mused. They were "somehow more impressed by familiar things in an unaccustomed setting than by really new and strange things." As they rode farther, these plains began to be covered by sisal plantations—the future, many thought, of the British East African economy. Demand for sisal, a type of agave with strong fibers used to make rope, cloth, and rugs, was growing. The fields that lay before them muted the landscape to the shade of the sisal's gray-green leaves.

The train next rode past Tsavo, where lions had once halted the building of the railway by their frequent attacks on humans who were working there. The tales they had heard of the lions of Tsavo instilled Martin and Osa with a sense that these "man-eaters" possessed "a boldness and cunning that seemed almost supernatural." Were the lions smart enough to know, Martin wondered, "that the completion of the railway would mean the ultimate destruction of the animal kingdom over which they held sway"?

As the train climbed in elevation toward the equator, the scenery and wildlife outside their window again transformed. The plains became dotted with mimosa and acacia trees in low scrubby clusters. Rivers wound through the landscape, and herds of zebras, wildebeests, baboons, and ostrich seemed to be

everywhere. The Johnsons caught quick glimpses of Mount Kilimanjaro, its peak covered in snow and "dazzling in the sun against
the clear, dark blue of the African sky." A group of seven giraffes
near the train raised a lump in Martin's throat: "[I]t is things like
that first glimpse of giraffes, not 'hair-breadth 'scapes' nor hand-
to-hand encounters, that mean adventure to me. They stood there
so unreal, so impossible—in spite of their ungainly forms, so beautiful." The land on this stretch was part of the newly established
Southern Game Reserve. Everything to the track's south was set
aside to preserve wildlife. Indeed, it seemed to Martin that on
the south side of the train, there were game "as far as the eye can
see," while on the north side there were fewer herds. "It was as if
they understood," he reflected, "that the railway was in a sense a
dead-line."

At Kiu the train stopped to refuel, and the Johnsons ate lunch
in another Harvey-esque dining hall. Though the houses here were
similar to those at Voi, the native people were completely different. The Maasai, as these people were known, carried *knobkerries*
(polished clubs) and feather-adorned spears, and wore clothing
only of animal skins. Earrings made of sticks and odd metal items
such as typewriter reels and safety pins hung heavily from their
ears, stretching their lobes well below their chins. Bracelets and
necklaces clung tightly to their skin. They were, according to Osa,
quite interesting people, yet she kept her distance from them as
they were "inexpressibly dirty" and surrounded by swarms of flies.

The Maasai, confessed Martin, "were of a type entirely new
to us . . . a strange, wild pastoral people." Members of the Maasai
tribes refused to recognize British rule and would not accept the
usual jobs of native people within the British system. They would
not pay taxes but did not openly fight British forces, so the colo-
nizers signed a land agreement with them allowing them to retain
their independent, nomadic lives and customs. Though they lost
large swaths of their former lands to settlers, the Maasai were the
only tribe in East Africa able to secure such diplomatic respect

from the British. Thus, some Maasai lived within Kenya's Southern Game Reserve, where they continued to raise sheep, goats, and small cattle. Because they were not a hunting tribe, the British believed the protection of wildlife would be further secured by their presence.

After Kiu, the train went straight to Nairobi through an "ever-changing, ever-interesting panorama." One depression of tall grass, they were told by a fellow passenger, was reportedly filled with lions. They strained their eyes to see the wild cats, but "[n]othing stirred the grasses save the wind." The promise of wildlife and the decreasing signs of human presence made Martin, Osa, and John feel they "were in wild country." Finally, they had arrived in the Africa of their imaginations.

Upon reaching Nairobi, Martin and Osa again felt the disorientation of the strange but familiar. The train station resembled those in the States, but the people were again wildly different. Dark-skinned porters dressed in long khaki shirts assisted with their luggage. Where Osa had expected a "squalid tropical village" she found a "clean, white, modern city." Most of Nairobi's population dressed in "good well-cut tailored woolens." She had expected them all to wear safari outfits with pith helmets every day and was surprised to see such cosmopolitanism in the wilds of Africa. Khaki-clad British officers walked the streets while white women in typical Western-style dress bustled along with children and their nannies, but it certainly was not a sea of khaki and white. Boer farmers were recognizable by their felt hats, Arabs wore traditional turbans and veils, and Indian men donned puffed pants and women wrapped themselves in a rainbow of silk saris. The streets were filled with a variety of life from around the globe, but Africa was evident in the red-fezzed *askaris* (native soldiers), servants dressed in flowing white robes the Johnsons called *konzas,* and market women wearing only animal hides.

At the time of the Johnsons' arrival, Nairobi was the government seat of British East Africa. Its white population was near two thousand. Vehicles as diverse as mule-drawn wagons, rick-shaws, and American automobiles crowded the streets. Office buildings and department stores—some five stories tall—lined the sidewalks. Taxis zipped down paved streets, and the Johnsons took one to their hotel, which had all the conveniences they needed, including electric lights. The mix of modern and frontier elements reminded Osa of "a pioneer town" where white men enjoyed a more agreeable climate than could be found by the humid African coast. Indeed, Nairobi's elevation of six thousand feet above sea level made for cooler tropical temperatures.

After a short stay in the hotel, Osa and her father-in-law found a bungalow outside town surrounded by an acre of "flowers familiar to our western eyes, as well as the brilliant unfamiliar blooms of the tropics." Martin was happy with the eight-room house but had the lease amended so he could add a darkroom. Osa was thrilled with the gardens. Roses, oranges, lemons, pineapples, guavas, bananas, apples, peaches, plums, and pears were already planted. Osa hired two Kikuyu men as gardeners who helped her plant a "kitchen-garden" with corn, lettuce, radish, bean, tomato, and pea seeds she had brought with her from Kansas. Kalowatt, too, enjoyed the gardens. She happily swung through the towering trees, finally free after long months in a New York City apartment. The tame gibbon ape fascinated the native people, who often watched her "antics" and began to refer to the Johnsons as "the people with the gibbon ape"—a distinctive designation, to be sure.

As was the custom in Nairobi, the Johnsons hired a crew of servants, including Aloni, the main house servant, and Zabenelli, the butler. To save money, the Johnsons hired nine others for part-time, divided work. Every servant came with his own assistant. Their cook's name was Joanna, but, thinking this "a trifle too feminine," the Johnsons took to calling him 'Mpishi—the Swahili word for cook. He was, according to Osa, "an enormous man with a wide grin and strong, white teeth" and "the aristocrat of the servants." He donned a smock and khaki shorts with "tattered socks, and a pair of cast-off shoes" that the Johnsons could not get him to change. On Sunday, however, he dressed in starched white pants and a straw hat that Osa thought made him "almost splendid."

Osa enjoyed managing the household and learning about the unfamiliar ways of the African people they had hired. She took Aloni's assistant, a twelve-year-old boy who was his son by a former wife, to market to carry her basket while she shopped. Osa frequented two markets in Nairobi, the "white market" and one run by native Africans and East Indians. The first, run by British and Boer farmers, fascinated Osa and John, who often accompanied her there. "It was just as much fun as a crossword puzzle, and almost as exciting as backgammon," Osa confessed, "for everything—butter, eggs, flowers, fruit, vegetables, tin ware, and furniture—was sold at auction." The second market offered inexpensive potatoes, alligator pears, strawberries, asparagus, and freshly butchered meat and wild game.

Though the Johnsons themselves had no trouble with wildlife in their Nairobi home, the wild sometimes penetrated the frontier town. Lions and leopards took down horses and dogs or lurked under porches. "Nearly every edition of the newspaper contained an animal accident story," they noticed. Headlines announced: "Hunter Mauled by Lion" and "Lone Settler Gored by Rhino." A stroll through the cemetery revealed nearly a dozen animal-related deaths inscribed on tombstones.

Fascinated by their eccentric new neighbors, many of Nairobi's noted British hunters and explorers called upon the Johnsons in their bungalow. They had heard from biologist Carl Akeley, the Explorers Club member who had encouraged the Johnsons to visit Africa, about Martin Johnson's mission to photograph Africa's disappearing wildlife. Explorer and photographer Maj. A. Radclyffe Dugmore became so familiar that Martin invited him to use his lab. The governor of Kenya, Maj. Gen. Sir Edward

Northey, visited often to share his views on wildlife conservation. He wished all people who came to Africa for wildlife experiences would use a camera instead of a gun. Stanley Taylor of the Bureau of Native Affairs taught the Johnsons about African cultures and let Martin store negatives in the bureau's vault, which was the only fireproof vault in all of Nairobi.

Staff at the Bureau of Native Affairs helped Martin carefully plan his "safari"—as all expeditions in the wilderness of Africa were called after the Swahili word *kusafiri,* meaning "to travel." The word derived from the days of East Africa's Arab slave and ivory traders, who would pierce the interior of the continent to obtain these valuable goods for market. Safari now referred to any expedition, whether by motorcar, oxcart, or mule and camel caravan. Martin consulted with Nairobi's best safari outfitter at the time, Tarlton, Whetham & Burman, for appropriate and capable men to bring along. He purchased two "safari Fords" from the local dealer, Newton Limited. One was a new model with a body designed specifically for camera supplies, and the other, previously owned, was custom outfitted per the Johnsons' specifications. Martin hired porters and oxcarts to carry the rest of their supplies. Finally, they hired two headmen, chief hired hands—Jerramani and Ferraragi—who came highly recommended by game warden A. Blayney Percival. Jerramani had guided Theodore Roosevelt's 1909 African safari. In preparation for the expedition, the Johnsons practiced their marksmanship. All safari leaders had to kill animals for meat to feed their crew, as Africans were not permitted to carry guns due to British laws created out of fears of African resistance. Some Africans, designated as "gun bearers," could carry a weapon for their employers but could not shoot it. Martin considered hiring a "white hunter" to take care of the meat, but the fee—$1,000 a month—more than any other single cost of personnel, was too extravagant.

Game warden A. Blayney Percival educated them on African wildlife and its habitats. He had been a game warden for twenty years and hated the influx of big-game hunters that had grown in recent years. At first, he was rather standoffish because he was suspicious that the Johnsons' intentions were similar. He thought most visitors to Kenya came only "to fatten their egos with trophies, no matter how obtained, and whose lust to kill would in time become a menace to African wildlife." One day, while Percival was over for tea and cake, he handed Martin an old, yellowed notebook written by a Scottish explorer who had traveled the region in the early nineteenth century. Along with descriptions of cameleopards and unicorns (just giraffes and oryx, according to Percival), the man wrote of a lake formed within a crater, "a sort of sanctuary," that remained unmapped and undisturbed by hunters. That it was unaffected by hunters was true, but the lake had long been known by several of the region's tribes and written about by American explorer Arthur Donaldson Smith in 1895. In their writings, Martin and Osa were intentionally vague about its location and omitted references, like Smith's visit, that might have helped lead people to it. They couched the lake in mystery and myth, speaking only of the legendary Scotsman's account and claiming that if natives knew of it, they never spoke of it. According to Percival's yellowed notebook, the lake was some five hundred miles "as the crow flies" north, along the Abyssinian border. (It actually lies at the top of Mount Marsabit.)

"I'd like to see you go there some day with your camera and come back with a record of what animals are really like in their natural, undisturbed state," Percival told Martin. Excited, the Johnsons said they would go right away, but Percival told them to pace themselves. The lake sat on the other side of a difficult landscape, including nearly 250 miles of the Kaisoot Desert, and they had yet to go on their first African safari. The lake was too big an undertaking for novices, no matter how ambitious, he insisted. Try a few smaller expeditions first, he advised. He then turned to Osa and cautioned, "if I were you, I wouldn't set my heart on going. It will be no trip for a woman." ("It seemed to me I must

On safari, Martin and Osa cleverly outfitted their automobiles for filming.

explode," Osa would later write in *I Married Adventure*. "No trip for a woman! That again!")

At Percival's advice, they decided their first safari would be to the Athi River, just thirty miles from Nairobi, where they could film herds of wildlife without being too far from help, if needed. Before leaving, Martin and Osa—who had never before driven motorcars—took driving lessons at Tarlton, Whetham & Burman, then passed their tests with the Nairobi police. During her test, Osa nearly hit a tree and drove directly into a squadron of askaris. The police gave her a license just to be rid of her (or so said Martin). All were wary of riding with her on the road—all save John, who sat by her side as they set out across the plains.

After only twenty minutes, they came to an expansive tract teeming with wildlife. Ostriches, zebras, and gazelles all "had a passion for racing with automobiles," said Martin, "a passion that seemed to be instinctive with animals throughout Africa. Something impels them to out distance you and cross the road in front of you. Then they are content to let you pass." Osa competed with the animals, veering off the road several times in the process. They arrived at the Athi River after four hours and set up camp beneath a grove of mimosa trees on the banks of a gentle stream. Throwing a heavy tarp over one of the Fords, they made a shelter and spent their first night in the African wilderness.

"It was our first evening in the African open," Osa remembered, "and I was fit to pop with excitement. I was even shivering a little." Knowing his cameras could capture neither darkness nor sound, Martin wished he were "a poet and could write verses about them. The mysterious pounding of invisible hoofs, the rush and thunder of herds across the plain, the grunt of the wildebeest, the sneeze of the hartebeest, the shrill, ridiculous yap, yap, yap of the common zebra, which barks like a dog; the boom-boom of the cock ostrich, which we took at first for the roar of a lion; the ghoulish laughter of hyenas . . ."

They awoke to wildlife milling about the riverbank, but in her rush and excitement, Osa tripped over their car tarp's guy rope and scared them all away. With nothing around to film, the Johnsons decided to go on their first African hunt to get meat for the crew. Ferraragi was ashamed to carry a woman's gun and was miffed by Osa's request to do so. Not ready to take any disobedience from a hired man, Martin not only forced him to carry Osa's gun but gave him the camera to boot. This was just the beginning of the difficulties of their first safari. Martin and Osa spent the day aiming at large herds of gazelle but did not fell a single specimen.

Martin, who did not like to hunt anyway, consoled himself by taking photographs of the Grant's gazelle. While this pleased the Johnsons, they were losing the confidence of their headmen. On the fourth day, Jerramani asked for a gun, saying the men were starving. When Martin refused, Jerramani seemed impressed with this assertion of leadership. The problem of fresh meat, however, was still unresolved so Martin went out with a .470 Bland elephant gun, which he did not know how to use, and pulled both triggers at once. This sent him reeling and broke the gun. Though Osa was a better shot and begged to go with him, Martin would not allow it. He knew his control over his crew was at stake. Martin returned that day with a kill, but the crew, he discovered, were Mohammedans, and they refused to eat animals that had not been properly "halalled" (referring to halal, food that has been prepared in accordance to Islamic law—in this case, killed by having their throats cut). On safari, however, they settled for meat that had come from an animal whose throat had been cut immediately after it had been shot, but Martin had not known, and it was too late.

Martin was discouraged. He was spending more time hunting than photographing and felt the dull pain of failure. Osa tried to help by going fishing, but she dropped her bait in the water and didn't catch a single fish, though she could see the river was full of them. John encouragingly chalked up these failures as learning experiences and the whole purpose of the trip in the first place. When they heard a lion roar later that night, the safari regained some of its excitement. "[The roar] had a strange, terrible beauty I cannot describe," said Martin. "It was like a deep-voiced melancholy trumpet reverberating over the plain. At times it seemed quite close; at times it was far off, a mere shadow of sound in the distance."

Giving up on hunting, Martin and Osa began the drive from camp to purchase halal meat in Nairobi (though Martin only admitted they were driving to Nairobi for bread, as 'Mpishi's loaves were hard as rocks). On the way Martin stopped to take footage of an antelope herd, telling Osa to fire her gun to "get a little action" for the film. Thinking of their meat problems, Osa aimed at the largest buck in sight and bagged it in one shot. Martin, assuming she shot without aiming for the purposes of the film, turned to her and joked: "I guess we're better when we don't take aim than when we do!" Osa insisted she had intended to hit the buck, but Martin did not believe her. She was furious. Though proud of having obtained the buck, she admitted to a tinge of hunter's regret: "The soft eyes of the lovely creature were wide open, and they seemed to look straight at me with reproach for taking his life." As she began to tear up, she sobbed to Martin, "I wish I hadn't killed him! . . . He's so harmless—and so beautiful."

Despite the fresh meat, the Johnsons soon packed up and headed back to Nairobi. Percival laughed at their trials and tribulations. It was typical, he said, to have trouble aiming guns and cameras in Africa. Everyone does. "I don't know whether it's the light or atmosphere," he told them, "but whatever it is, it's almost impossible to aim or focus accurately until you're accustomed to it." Martin realized now they were not ready for the unmapped lake. They needed more time and more practice with both guns and cameras. Percival said he'd let them know when he thought they were ready.

So Martin could concentrate on his aim with the cameras, for their next safari he hired an old white hunter, John Walsh, for five dollars a day, which included the use of his house near the Athi Plains, about forty miles from Nairobi. With renewed optimism, the Johnsons again set out in their safari Fords across the wildlife-filled plains. Because they did not need as much gear this time, they left the porters behind. When they arrived at Walsh's place, however, they could not believe their eyes. It was nothing but a "two-room shanty of galvanized sheet iron" filled with old clothes and boots, empty alcohol bottles, yellowed newspapers from the 1890s, British dime novels, and several harmonicas. "I don't know," said Osa, "when I had seen anything as bleak, unless it was Mr. Walsh himself." He seemed a specimen of the frontier. He had, described Martin, "the uncanny air that living the wild, lonely life of the open often gives to men."

The car Walsh used to guide them was no better. It was "a demon Ford" they were convinced was "possessed of satanic power." Martin wondered at its ability to navigate the plains. "It was all but falling to pieces," he said, "but when [Walsh] got into it and went tearing off in pursuit of a herd of antelopes, it fairly leaped across that stony, grassy, bumpy plain, as if possessed." This mode of transport was not only harrying, but unfruitful. The noise from Walsh's vehicle scared the animals away, so there were none left for Martin to photograph. Walsh did not seem to realize this was a problem for photographic hunting. Feeling a bout of stubbornness mixed with failure, one day Martin went out to a blind alone. He sat there for hours. At one point, so excited by a group of warthogs, he took four hundred feet of film. He later admitted that twenty-five feet would have been sufficient for these generally uninteresting creatures, but he was just happy to be shooting something. His patience paid off, however. A group of impala later came near enough to the blind for Martin to photograph as well.

At dinner that night—a feast that included a Thomson's gazelle Osa shot—Walsh told them of caves haunted by leopards and cheetahs. Their interest ignited, the Johnsons decided to go to the spot at dawn. In the morning, however, Walsh was stricken with a flare-up of malaria, so they set out for the caves without him. Along the way, Martin spotted a leopard eating a zebra kill. He set up his camera and waited for light when Walsh, apparently feeling better, approached and scared the leopard away. They continued on, seeing a herd of wild dogs and hyena that, despite Martin's aversion to hunting, he thought were worth shooting on sight. Hyenas, he explained, hunt in packs and will attack both wild game and livestock. They are, Martin opined, "the lowest and meanest of all creation. . . . [The hyena] is as yellow as his ugly striped coat" and kills for "the sake of killing." "[T]he hyena nature is apparent in every line of his body," he explained describing how this pack "came slinking along on their bellies, tails between their legs, looking at us malevolently out of their green eyes, snarling and showing their long yellow teeth, but giving never a sign of fight."

Martin built another camera blind, where he and Osa headed at dusk. Zebra, impala, kongoni, and ostrich wandered past, but not close enough to photograph. After three days crouched in the blind, Osa's knees ached, and she lost her patience with the process. Walsh was feeling better but "had washed his hands of us" and went hunting alone for meat to sell at the market in Nairobi. The next day, Osa stayed behind with Kalowatt. She tried to get a gazelle for dinner but had to content herself with cooking tinned meat and vegetables instead.

Though this second safari went more smoothly than the first, Martin returned to Nairobi with only his warthog and impala pictures. Percival assured him he was "getting on to the peculiarities of the atmosphere now" and that in only one or two more tries, he would "be ready for anything"—including the mysterious lake. Percival directed the couple to another area for a short expedition—the Ithanga Hills, which lay northeast of Nairobi. As John was anxious to see wild lions, rhinoceroses, buffaloes, and leopards, they all agreed to the wildlife-rich locale. Percival recommended they stay at the Whitehead Plantation while exploring the area, but Martin refused. He wanted to rough it on "a real safari."

With their personal servants and a dozen porters, the Johnsons began the journey to the Ithanga Hills. They sent ox wagons filled with camp equipment and chop boxes ahead and drove the safari Fords to Thika—a resort used by the white population of Nairobi as the jumping-off point for safaris in the North Country. They stayed at the Blue Posts Hotel, overlooking the Chania and Thika Rivers and Falls. The hotel was a comfortable assemblage of grass huts built in the native style. The town itself contained more Western-style houses alongside native tin huts, Indian *dukas* (shops), and a general store.

The next day, they were off into the North Country with their ox wagons, porters, and cars climbing slowly. They drove through fields of sisal as they neared the Whitehead Plantation, "an outpost," Martin said, "of England in the African wild." The Whitehead bungalow was surrounded by a flower garden that reflected to Osa "the culture and charm of our host and hostess." Though enchanted with such domestication, they had already decided not to stay here, and Osa looked forward to being in the wilderness.

Despite the comforts of the plantation, Martin wanted to keep to his plan for "a real safari," so they drove another four miles north, where the wildlife would be more abundant. As John supervised the camp setup, Osa and Martin went scouting with Jerramani. The hills and vegetation reminded them of a New England forest, with neatly lined trees growing from sparse underbrush. They walked for about an hour before coming to the rim of a crater that formed a "natural stadium some ten miles across and twenty-five miles long." Everywhere they saw game trails, but no wildlife. "We went carefully along, looking to right and left, hoping to meet the great beasts—and hoping not to meet them," said Martin.

Jerramani led them down a "dark, cool, and mysterious" ravine where they came upon wild buffaloes asleep under a tree. Martin snuck around with his camera to within one hundred feet and began turning the crank. Osa watched in fear and anticipation. The lighting seemed perfect for photography, but Martin's nerves interfered. "It was hard for me to turn it at a uniform speed," Martin said. At the sound of the crank, the buffaloes awoke and jumped to their feet. They began to paw at the ground. Martin turned to Osa and told her she must shoot the leader if they began to charge. All stood frozen—buffaloes and humans. "The sun glistened on their black hides and turned their eyes to blood-red balls of fire," Martin said, recalling Carl Akeley's opinion that despite fantastic tales of lion and rhinoceros ferocity, buffaloes were the most dangerous animals in Africa.

It was unclear whether Jerramani's voice or Osa's scream set the scene back in motion, but before they knew it, Martin and Osa were sprinting back up the ravine. Jerramani watched them, clearly disappointed in their cowardice. They ran all the way back to camp while Jerramani walked slowly to express his disgust. "It shamed and irritated me," said Martin, "that I was not a hero to my gun-bearer." He was determined to prove himself so Jerramani could return to Nairobi able to brag about the bravery of his bwana (Swahili for "boss"). Though Jerramani was technically an employee, Martin felt the need to prove his masculinity to this man, whose culture required a certain kind of bravery.

Martin, Osa, and Jerramani returned to a comfortable camp—their first full safari setup. There was a tent for sleeping with a lined, double roof for extra sun protection. Attached to this was a small room with a canvas tub. Two canvas easy chairs awaited them, perfect for collapsing into after their long walks. A larger tent for dining was crafted of tarpaulin, and one tent served as storage for the photographic equipment. The porters built accommodations for the headmen, who preferred grass huts to canvas tents. The porters themselves slept outside by the fire. Kalowatt slept in her usual box but freely swung among the trees in the daytime. The porters grew to love and hate the ape's playfulness, as she jumped from their shoulders, stole their skullcaps, and hung them from the nearest tree. They called her alternately *memsahib's toto* (missus's baby) and the daughter of Satan. "The wilderness," thought Martin, "went to her head."

Martin, determined to get better footage of wildlife in the Ithanga Hills, told Jerramani he wanted to take some of the porters with them so they could scare buffaloes toward the camera and within range of his lens. They set out to find a herd with Osa and John manning the guns. Soon they came to a herd. Martin set up his camera, telling Osa to be ready to scream at their approach in case the guns did not scare the animals away. "It's the best ammunition we have," he told her. As he had planned, the men scared the buffaloes toward the camera, and Osa shot two of them, causing the herd to change direction and ensuring their safety. Martin proudly took Osa in his arms, happy at her quick shot and glad that he could now have confidence in her ability to protect him from oncoming wildlife. For dinner they ate the buffalo Osa felled. The thrilled porters and servants sat singing around the fire until quite late in "strange, monotonous, rhythmic

melodies" that ceased only when Jerramani told them their bwanas were about to turn in.

Filled with the history of adventure, the landscape of the
Ithanga Hills had hosted Paul Rainey, Major Dugmore, Theodore
Roosevelt, and Lady Mackenzie (the first woman to lead a safari in
the region). Martin and Osa slid down the bowl of the crater and
walked through the forest. Near dusk, a herd of a hundred buffaloes threatened to charge but wheeled and ran off at the last minute. They stopped to camp, and Martin filtered water in his usual
method—boiling, adding alum and potash, then boiling again—to
prevent waterborne diseases.

The next morning, Martin awoke suddenly to the noise of men
running and yelling. He went outside the tent and asked Jerramani,
who had Kalowatt clinging to his neck, what had happened. Jerramani pointed to a tree trunk, in which was lodged a feathered
arrow. Apparently a native had taken aim at Kalowatt and tried to
shoot him for food. The porters, who had gone off in search of the
culprit, returned with the native shooter, who wore only a dirty
animal skin over his shoulder. "He was a scrawny, wild-looking
little man," said Martin. Aloni took the man's quiver, which was
full of similar feathered arrows. The man was from the Dorobo
('Ndorobo) people, who lived in the forest and whom the Johnsons had heard a great deal about. They were supposedly "the most
primitive of the East African natives," living in caves and surviving
on game and wild honey alone. Other African natives, the Johnsons observed, looked down upon the Dorobo as "the 'poor black
trash' of Africa."

Martin, however, found the man fascinating. He asked him
to stay to help them track game and gave him a bowl of "mealy-
meal" (mielie-meal), a porridge made from corn. Jerramani did not
approve of giving handouts to the Dorobo. The next morning the
man was gone. He returned the following day, however, reporting
that he had seen a leopard near their camp. He led them to the spot,
where Martin proceeded to set up his cameras. Osa and Ferraragi

searched the area for signs of leopard, and after a while Osa put her hand up, signaling that she saw the animal in the bushes. Ferraragi handed her a gun, and she shot. The leopard leaped toward the camera quickly before retreating and hiding under a tree.

"The thought of recording that spring in motion-pictures," said Martin, "made me forget all the stories I had heard of maulings received by men from leopards." Osa again approached the leopard and, before signaling to Martin, shot the animal. Martin angrily abandoned his camera. "You have spoiled my picture," he yelled at her. But Osa showed him that she had wounded the animal with her first shot, and he would not have sprung again anyway. She had merely put the animal out of its misery. Back at camp, their hired skinner, Japanda, removed the leopard pelt while the rest of the men sang, thrilled with the bravery and skill of their bwanas. Martin gave the Dorobo man a shilling, and he left the next day.

Sometimes using gunshots to scare animals into action for the camera backfired. Martin had wanted to get footage of this leopard leaping toward the camera, so Osa had to scare it toward him. However, when the animal seemed too close to Martin, Osa felt she had to protect him. Her humanity obligated her to put the animal out of its misery when she accidentally wounded it. Martin and Osa often described killing animals in the course of their filming as self-defense, and they received little criticism for this method because of their greater intentions. At a time when most Hollywood films used staged or caged animals, their films were among the first to show wild animals in their native habitats and were praised for their authenticity. However, capturing such footage required that the Johnsons place themselves in some danger and, consequently, occasionally kill charging animals. Conservationists of the time were not likely to publicly criticize a project that was bringing awareness of African wildlife to audiences and spreading the message of conservation. Killing to protect one's life did not undermine that message.

After a rainy day in camp, the Johnsons set out to find more wildlife to photograph. They came across fresh spoor and tracks hinting of two rhino nearby. They followed the tracks but after an hour lost them, with no rhino in sight. Stopping to rest under the shade of a mimosa tree, they told the men they had taken along to split up and look in all directions for the rhinoceroses. After an hour there was no sign of either men or rhinos, so Osa, Martin, Jerramani, and Kavairondo (who carried their cameras) began exploring the area themselves. Suddenly, Jerramani halted and touched Martin's arm. "Simba, simba," he whispered in Swahili, indicating a lion was nearby. Then Martin saw it—a large lion lying only fifty yards in front of them under a sparse covering of bushes, feeding on a zebra kill. The lion's back was turned to them, but it quickly pivoted to face them. "For one marvelous second," Martin disclosed, "he stood, fierce and beautiful, his front feet on the zebra he had killed, glaring at us with savage, yellow-green eyes. I watched him, motionless with admiration." Osa had other, more practical ideas. As the lion turned, she grabbed her gun and fired. Osa was a bit quick with her gun during their early days in Africa. Like many who visited there for the first time, she was excited about the novelty of trophy hunting in Africa (they had gained permits to take several animals). She was also likely a bit fearful of not shooting. If she was not aggressive with the gun, Martin might be mauled, or worse. Once she understood wildlife behavior better, she did not shoot so hastily.

Martin turned to find Kavairondo had set up the camera. Excited, Martin began to film the dying lion, who bared his teeth and tried to lunge at them. He was too wounded to attack, however. Osa watched with excitement. "Isn't he a beauty!" she remarked, admiring his long, black mane. The lion snarled, roared, and tried to spring in what Martin thought "a marvelous exhibition of animal courage and endurance. . . . Right there, I gave the lion precedence over all the beasts for bravery, and I never had cause to reverse my decision." When the lion closed its eyes for the last time, Martin blew a whistle, and his porters came, shouting with excitement. "We marched home to a barbaric chant, in which we distinguished the words *memsa-hib* and *simba,* many times repeated," said Martin. "In many of the native tribes of Africa a man is not proved a man until he has killed a lion. We had to bring home the King of Beasts before we could prove ourselves worthy masters. . . . It was Osa that had brought down the lion, but I had my full share of the glory. After all, she was my woman." While it is easy to wonder how Martin was affected by Osa's astute hunting, he seems to be a proud husband rather than a man with a wounded ego.

On the way back to camp, they paused to photograph a few bushbucks grazing in the light of the setting sun. Osa thought they looked beautiful and tame, and wanted to make a pet of one. Her encounters with wildlife wavered between the thrill of the hunt and the desire to nurture. As Martin and Osa watched the peaceful scene, John saw another creature, and pointed his gun toward something moving in the bushes. Osa saw him taking aim and crept around to see what it was. John said he saw something yellowish in color and thought it might be a lion, but it wasn't. It was a leopard, and it instantly leaped directly toward Martin and his camera. Fearing for his safety, Osa shot and the animal fell. Rather than being relieved, Martin complained that she shot animals before he had a chance to film them.

Despite their general good luck in the Ithanga Hills, they broke down their safari a few days early. They had run out of salt and had withstood "two days of choking, tasteless food" before "we could not stand it any longer." In the heat of Africa, where hydration was difficult, "salt was like water to a man dying of thirst in the wilderness." But they headed home feeling more satisfied with their fitness for safari than they had after their previous expedition.

When they reunited with Percival in Nairobi, he invited them to join him on an inspection of the Southern Game Reserve.

Osa and Blayney Percival clearly enjoying their safari.

Rumor had it that elephants were migrating through the area, which excited the adventurer and the photographer in Martin. No one yet understood why elephants migrated. Though hunters and natives had theories and opinions based on their experiences, the scientific community had not studied the matter thoroughly. Martin thought some photographic footage of the event might win more support for his work from serious scientific parties.

They all boarded the train for Kiu, where they slept in the station as guests of the game-reserve patrol. The patrol consisted of six Maasai who Percival said were the best game wardens because of their traditions, which allowed for little killing of wildlife. Each patrolman wore a red blanket draped over one shoulder. The headman, Nakuru, wore khaki shorts, rolled puttees (cloth wound around the leg from the ankle to the knee, for support and protection), a worn jacket, and a cap with a visor and earflaps.

The following morning, the Johnsons, Percival, and the game wardens trekked through the plains in the brutal rays of the sun.

They saw silhouettes of giraffes in the distance. Herds of zebras, antelopes, wildebeests, gnus, and elands dotted the plains, which otherwise reminded Osa of Texas or the Dakotas. Everywhere they saw dried rhinoceros skulls and bones. Percival explained that the area was filled with such remains left over from the wanton slaughter of rhinos during recent warfare. He believed no rhinoceroses remained on that land at the time.

After a full morning on the plains, they reached forests of mimosa and acacia trees. When they came upon the dried bed of the Old Garai River, they stopped to make camp. While the porters and servants set up the campsite, they searched nearby and found elephant tracks less than a day old. However, they had no luck finding the elephant and returned after two hours.

At night Martin and Osa lay awake, listening to the chorus of roaring lions. "Somehow it had never occurred to me that there would be so many in one place, not even in Africa," said Osa. "I hoped I didn't look as nervous as I felt, but at any rate Percival tried to reassure me and said there weren't really very many, that it just sounded that way because they were circling us from curiosity, trying to figure us out."

The idea of lions circling their camp did nothing to soothe Osa's nerves. She lay awake, trying to distinguish individual roars. "One had a particularly deep, long-drawn, sepulchral tone of which I'm sure he was very proud," Osa commented. "It had a rain-barrel quality that was magnificent and spine-chilling, and I visualized him as a great, tawny beast sporting a fine, heavy mane and surrounded by a coterie of admiring lionesses." After a few days they grew accustomed to the roaring, but, Martin admitted, the sound still sent shivers down his spine. "There was in that shiver," he remarked, "not only fear but a pleasurable realization of the wilderness."

Despite the eerie evening sounds, the Johnsons awoke ready to track not lions, but African elephants. On the way they came across the largest herd of giraffes they had yet seen—thirty-seven of them.

Martin used his telephoto lens to get a shot as they stampeded over a hilltop. They then returned to the elephant tracks, following them to a native village. The people there reluctantly informed them they were too late. The herd had left a week ago. They turned back toward camp. Martin stopped to photograph elands, which Percival told them were disappearing due to overhunting. They were quite fortunate to see them now, he believed, saying they would probably not "ever again see so many, all in one group."

Within the protective borders of the game reserve, wildlife was more abundant. Every day Martin and Osa were learning the value of the reserve, and they were learning from Percival things they did not learn on their own safaris—most of all that wildlife there was threatened, even when it seemed abundant. Percival lobbied for game reserves and struggled to maintain some of them against expanding settlement. "Civilized men and wild creatures, men or animals, cannot live as neighbors without a clash of interests," said Martin, "and when such a clash occurs, it is almost inevitably the interests of the wild creatures that are sacrificed." They all agreed. Even if farmers didn't harm herds, "Every fence you build is a stroke in the death-knell of the antelopes and gazelles and zebras that must run wild and free or else perish," Martin lamented.

East African settlers, however, did not support the reserves. Martin explained their argument that British East Africa was not "nature's zoo." "The game must go to make room for men," they believed. But the reserves, Percival argued, were not desirable agricultural lands, and there was plenty more fertile land available elsewhere. "They are simply possessed by the mania for 'civilizing' the country," critiqued Martin, "and so they say, 'The game must go.'" Under Percival's guidance, Martin and Osa came to understand the problem of preservation in East Africa and began to feel less excitement at the thrill of the hunt and chase. They were developing a wildlife ethic and, inspired by Percival, began to perceive that their mission was not merely to film wildlife before it disappeared, but to use their experiences and films to keep wildlife from disappearing. Their images, they now believed, could educate people about wildlife and the need for conservation.

Unable to catch up with the elephant herds, the Johnsons decided to remain at camp instead and set up a blind near the river. The first blind Martin built was a failure, and Percival told him to set it up closer to the water, which Martin thought would scare the animals away. But Percival assured him that in the reserve, animals were used to people, particularly the Maasai herdsmen who did them no harm, and were thus not afraid of humans. Martin sat in the blind and watched Maasai herdsmen water their cattle all morning. In the afternoon, wildlife came to the riverbank. Zebras, kongonis, impalas, gnus, elands, and warthogs drank and milled about. Martin observed leaders in each herd, who moved forward, checking for safety, before the rest followed.

The animals pawed the ground to make water holes in the dry riverbed. Different species stood near each other but did not intermingle. Martin enjoyed watching the animals play: "The zebras gamboled about and nipped one another . . . in mock battle," he observed, while the "gnus played tag in and out among the other animals." Not one animal noticed or seemed to care about Martin's blind or the noise of the camera. Their only fear, Martin concluded, was lions. And he did not "look or sound like a lion to them."

Martin had the men dig a water hole outside the blind to lure animals even closer. Osa set up a camera at a different angle from another blind while Percival took still photographs with an old camera. This footage, Martin thought, was among the best ever taken in Africa. They alternated days between the blinds with exploring the plains and Maasai villages, which also intrigued Osa and Martin. The people lived in huts built of dung and arranged around a square. Each night, the Maasai herdsmen drove their cattle and long-eared black goats into the square. Around the outside of the houses, thornbushes served as a fence, and a single watchman stood guard through the night to protect them from lion and leopard attacks. Martin was especially impressed by the

Zebra and wildebeest mingle in front of the lens at one of the many waterholes Martin and Osa visited for photographs.

Maasai code of bravery, which required every boy to spear a lion before he could be considered a man. "Bravery is a prime virtue among the Maasai," Martin said. "I had the greatest respect for every man I saw wearing [*sic*] proudly the lion's mane head-dress that proclaimed his manhood." Martin, and many of his contemporaries, depicted the Maasai as noble hunters. They did not hunt to excess. Rather, this ritual hunt nurtured a strong connection between man and the natural world. Hunting a lion with a spear is quite a different thing than driving up in a safari car and pointing a gun out its window. The Maasai spear hunt taught boys about lion behavior and fostered a sense of respect for the "king of beasts."

After a while, Percival was called back to Nairobi on business. He left the camp set up for Martin and Osa so they could continue their filming. They found, however, the orderly running of things was due largely to Percival's presence. Once Percival had left, the porters grew lazy, and one night they let the fire go out. (Safari camps burned fires through the night to keep animals, especially lions, away.) Martin awoke that evening to find a lion prowling about the camp. He blew his whistle to wake Jerramani and ordered the men to rebuild the fire, but there was no more wood. In Percival's absence, the men had ceased to even perform the most necessary of their usual tasks, and now lions were circling the camp. Martin put Jerramani and Ferraragi on guard the rest of the night.

In the morning, Martin lectured Jerramani and Ferraragi in broken Swahili. Jerramani laughed under his breath at Martin's effort to speak their language. To insult them even further, Martin left them in camp and took two other men as gun bearers when he and Osa went into the field for photographs. When they returned, there was a huge pile of wood prepared. "Plenty of wood, bwana?" Jerramani asked, holding back laughter. Martin did not want to joke, but he was amused at the size of the pile. He replied calmly, "It will do."

Percival's messenger came back to camp, reporting he would not be able to return as he had hoped, so the Johnsons packed up and headed toward Kiu. Along the way, they met a Maasai who had speared a lion, but the wounded animal had run off. He asked the safari to help him find the lion, but the Johnsons refused; they knew better. Percival had warned them against tracking wounded animals, which were often more aggressive in their weakened state. The next day, Osa was walking ahead of the rest of the party and chased after two lions. Martin called after her to stop. They had promised to only shoot in self-defense, and she was pursuing these animals for sport. Osa stopped and looked at him, puzzled, asking if he was afraid. She listened to his rational explanation but was not in agreement with his conservative spirit. Osa rather enjoyed the thrill of the hunt.

Back in Nairobi, the Johnsons looked for information on migrating elephants they might be able to film. Some were apparently migrating near the Amala River, about two hundred miles southwest of town. Wasting no time, they packed their equipment and struck out with their two Fords and a truck, with just a few men to assist. They camped that night at a town called Quarantine in the Kedong Valley, where cattle used to stop to be tested for disease. At sunset the surrounding hills turned a deep shade of red, and the game grazed peacefully around them.

They were up early the next morning, anxious to catch up with the elephants, but the old Ford wouldn't start. Their mechanic, Cotter, whom Martin praised as "a genius with engines," worked on it all morning, but it took until noon to get it running. They started toward the hills at the peak of the day's heat. Not only was the intense sun nearly unbearable, it boiled the water in the car radiators too quickly in an area where water was scarce. They had to stop the cars several times to let them cool down. When they reached the hills, they shifted to low gear and climbed for twenty-five miles uphill before meeting with a group of descending English prospectors whose Ford was steaming even worse than theirs. Though they had little to spare, they gave the men some water for their car. When night fell, the Johnsons camped without a drop of water for themselves, conserving it all for the Fords. In the morning, they drove on, but before reaching the top of the hills, the cars were again dry and they had to pour spoonfuls from a muddy pool into their radiators to get by.

Much relieved to get themselves and their vehicles to Narok, the next settlement, without incident, they enjoyed lunch with the district commissioner. In the afternoon, they reached the Southern Guaso Nyiro River, where they set up camp and enjoyed catfish that Osa caught for dinner. They reached the Loita plains the next day, driving through herds of animals and resisting the urge to stop for photographs. They had already lost precious time trying to catch up with the elephants. At half past three, they reached a fork in the road. Unsure which way to go, Martin went ahead to ask. He found the district commissioner and ranger on their way back from seeing the very elephants they were tracking down. The men were sad to report the main group had left the area. They may catch some stragglers, they told Martin, but that would be all. To help them get there quickly, the commissioner gave Martin his Maasai guide, who could lead them to the Amala River before nightfall.

Martin turned his car around and drove back toward the safari with the Maasai. Once they rejoined the group, the guide led them down the correct road toward the Amala River. When a snake crossed the road, Martin slammed on the brakes. It was twelve feet long, a mamba, the guide said, a relative of the cobra. Martin shot at the snake twice but missed, and it crawled into a hole beneath a tree stump. They tried to coax it out so Martin could kill it, but it did not budge. Martin said: "I was anxious to kill it; for it is a vicious enemy of men and animals. . . ." The road narrowed into a Maasai cattle road with logs strewn across that had to be removed by hand in order to get the cars through. All around them, broken tree branches showed the signs of elephants feeding. They reached the Amala River by dark and camped in a forest Martin and Osa found comfortingly similar to those of the American Midwest.

The Maasai guide was an askari—the only native Africans the British allowed to use guns. He did not, however, own his own weapon. One day, he asked Martin if he could borrow one while he went to visit a nearby village. He returned the next morning with some villagers who said they would assist with the elephant search. The men jumped onto the running boards of the cars and took hold while Martin and Osa drove where they directed them, but they found no elephants. For two more days the Maasai guide led them around, always going to nearby villages where he was greeted by friends. Martin began to wonder at the guide's sincerity. Was he helping them find elephants or taking advantage of the free ride and rifle? Martin had Zabenelli confront the Maasai, telling him to lead them to elephants or they would leave him behind. The next day the guide reported the elephants were just three miles from camp. Martin and Osa listened to him and crossed the plains to the edge of the forest, where they heard from within "the most fiendishly shrill cry you can imagine." This was the elephant's sound of alarm. The Maasai had led them upwind of the feeding elephants, and they caught the human scent before the Johnsons had a chance to see them. Martin and Osa grabbed their guns and stood watching the trees move with the elephants' motion. They heard them crash for over an hour but discovered they were running away rather than coming closer. Hopeful, they remained in the area for three more days but did not see or hear the elephants again.

As they headed back to Nairobi, they kept hearing rumors of migrating elephants in the area, but every time they went exploring, they found none. Martin was growing frustrated with Jerramani, who seemed to be knowingly leading them along tracks that were several days old in an attempt to pretend he knew what he was doing. This nighttime roar of lions made Martin switch gears. They stayed in one camp for a few days, trying to get footage of lions from a *boma*, or blind, in a tree. As night fell, they were startled by every noise and shadow and now worried about the elephants returning. "Much as we wanted to see elephants," said Martin, "we had no desire to be caught in a tree in a dark forest by a herd of the great animals." At eleven o'clock, they headed back to camp with all their equipment. Though the camp was only a mile away, it took them two hours to find it in the dark. They wandered in circles, hearing lions all around them. When they did find the camp, they saw the fire was low, and Martin woke the men to scold them.

The next day, they drove through plains with tame herds grazing or gathering around water holes. Stopping to film from a blind, Martin got some footage of the herds and caught his first glimpse of a wild rhinoceros. He was too far away to capture it on film, but the experience was nonetheless a thrilling one. The plains animals seemed to Martin "tamely wild," an idea he cultivated. Wildness did not, he thought, necessarily mean an animal was ferocious. A truly wild animal was one that had such little contact with humans that it did not know enough to fear them.

———

Osa and Martin stayed in Nairobi for four weeks as they prepared for their long-awaited, and hard-earned, safari to the unmapped lake. When they had their belongings neatly packed into sixty-pound bundles (the legal limit for porters), they headed north through the Kaisoot Desert toward the Abyssinian (now Ethiopian) border. Although Martin's father, John, wished to go all the way to the lake, he did not feel he would be able to, so he planned to only accompany them to the edge of settlement in the region. Along with their two safari Fords and truck, they hired four ox wagons, each with twelve oxen, and sent them a week ahead because they moved at a slower pace. They would meet in Meru, two hundred miles away by road (though only ninety miles "as the crow flies," Martin pointed out), and hire porters from the surrounding hills. Their party included Jerramani, Ferraragi, Zabenelli, 'Mpishi, Aloni, twelve "experienced safari men from Nairobi"—and, of course, Kalowatt, the gibbon ape.

They rested for two days in Thika, then set out with palpable excitement. Martin drove one Ford with Zabenelli, while Osa got behind the wheel of the other, carrying John and 'Mpishi. The mechanic Bud Cotter drove the truck with Aloni and Kalowatt. "We set out full of elation," Martin remembered. "We could not drive fast, for our Fords were so heavily loaded that we feared to break an axle, but we would not have driven fast if we could. There was too much that was new and interesting to see." Their path took them through rolling hills with tree-lined streams, and swamps filled with cane grass. Though there were not many animals visible, they saw more native people than they had yet encountered, as they were driving through the populous Kikuyu country. All the villages were similar in size, containing only three or four huts, mostly hidden by the tall grasses that blended with the huts' grass roofs. Native women carried heavy loads of produce on top of their heads, while the men accompanying them carried nothing at all. This made John particularly irate as the division of labor was seemingly so different from his familiar gentlemanly courtesy, and Martin thought the men "dandies" because of their elaborate body painting and decoration. They stopped to browse native markets filled mostly with animal hides and fresh vegetables, and Indian stores, or dukas, made of tin and grass.

Driving past one village, they came to a meeting of some three hundred Kikuyu men sitting in a large circle. Though they appeared to be just talking, they were wearing ostrich plume headdresses and holding spears—signs they were warriors. The men were nearly naked but had hides draped on their bodies and red clay streaks on their skin. Martin pulled over and set up his camera. While filming, another group of Kikuyu ran toward him, gesturing wildly. Zabenelli recounted what had happened: A young chief had forcibly taken the place of an elder. The three hundred Kikuyu they saw in the circle were the elder chief and his loyal followers. While Martin filmed, the young chief and his followers approached the gathering, and the crowd suddenly turned into a "wild, savage uproar" of six hundred Kikuyu warriors. Martin and Osa ran for the cars and watched while the chiefs appeared to come to some kind of truce. Just as quickly, the two factions ran toward their cars, asking for baksheesh—a payment for letting them film. Martin did not want to stop, so he threw pennies out the window, which the Kikuyu scrambled to pick up, eliminating, he thought, any semblance of dignity they previously had.

As the Johnsons approached Fort Hall, they caught glimpses of the snowcapped peak of 17,057-foot Mount Kenya, rumored to hold many elephants in its expansive forests. Government officials at Fort Hall offered them milk and eggs from their modest bamboo, mud, and grass houses. Their ox wagons had already moved on, traversing the western route around Mount Kenya. The officials recommended, however, that the cars take the better, but longer, road around the eastern side of the mountain through the town of Embu. The next morning at sunrise, they began this particularly challenging but scenic leg of their travels. "As we bowled along, the glaciers at the top of Mount Kenya, at first steely blue, took on the rose of the sun rising behind us," said Martin. "But we soon reached the flank of the mountain and, beginning to climb slowly up its side, exchanged the distant view of the snowcap for the nearer but no less lovely vistas." The rugged scenery reminded them of the Rockies but seemed even more wild. They saw more Kikuyus, many of them warriors, who stood right in the middle of the road as the cars approached to prove they were unfazed. The women, however, hid immediately. Young boys ran excitedly after the cars, shouting "Jambo, bwana!" ("Hello, mister!") Martin and Osa took their time over this pleasant stretch, taking pictures of the villages and the views.

They made the thirty-three miles to Embu, arriving after dark. This settlement was similar to Fort Hall, serving as support for white coffee and sisal farmers settled on the fertile slopes of Mount Kenya. As they departed for Meru the next day, officials asked them to give a ride to a young boy who had wandered into town from Meru. They took him in one of the cars, and he excitedly called to people on the streets to show them his good fortune.

The road wound through the mountains, turning at "the most astonishing caprices" though "splendid stretches of forest." Waterfalls seemed near enough to touch and plummeted a thousand feet. The cars puttered up steep inclines and "coasted down precipitous grades with our loads pushing us almost out of control." Their weight tested poorly constructed bridges. Their driving skills were tested by "hairpin curves that left no room for bad judgment or error of any sort." The rough roads wore on their bodies. When she got out of the car, Osa found her knees crumpled. "My muscles set up an involuntary shaking," she said, "and were numb at the same time."

After resting their aching bones, the next day they climbed

through what were to Osa "fairy-tale forests with foliage of such brilliant and varied greens as I have seen nowhere else in the world." As they approached Meru, the forest gave way to clearings, native gardens, and banana plantations, some on steep hillsides that would seem to make farming a rather dangerous occupation. Squads of teenage girls were repairing the roads. They ran excitedly at the cars, hopping on for a brief but thrilling ride. As the Johnsons drove through this pleasant country, Martin was struck by the differences between Africans and South Seas natives. "Melanesia is a gloomy, haunted place of dense and stinking jungle, of heavy tropical air; its inhabitants are cruel and treacherous and degraded," he noted. "Africa," by contrast, "is a land of sun and clean air, and its people are cheery, happy children." His praise of the African landscape as bright and healthy was a contrast to accounts by earlier explorers that portrayed "darkest Africa."

Though Martin was expressing contemporary racial stereotypes, he did not mean to belittle Africans or their cultures. His description of them as childlike was not meant to demean their intelligence, for Martin had great respect for the knowledge of the natural world many of them possessed. Rather, Martin meant to humanize them. Martin and Osa often depicted themselves "at play" in Africa, as well.

They arrived at Meru and found it the most pleasant of the British East African government stations they had yet seen. It stood on a plateau in front of the dense forest beyond. Houses were fronted by green lawns, and there was even a golf course and polo field carved from the forest. "White men, especially Englishmen, exiled in out-of-the-way parts of the world, have a way of trying to reconstruct a bit of the home land in the midst of a strange environment," Martin and Osa observed. "In a country abounding with beautiful native fabrics, the drawing-rooms of the English residents will have curtains of chintz imported from Manchester. No matter how they may differ in architecture and surrounding from the typical English dwelling, there is always something vaguely reminiscent of an English country-house about the British residences and plantation homes in the tropics."

The official in charge at Meru was Commissioner Crampton. He hosted the Johnsons in tents while they looked for elephants, but they remained unlucky in this regard. As they walked around the area, they saw native gardens ruined by the animals and houses abandoned due to their stampedes. This, they were told, happened every year when the herds came through. The people would run from the danger but always came back to rebuild and repair. The Johnsons' oxcarts arrived two weeks later, and they all camped outside of town. Crampton helped them find porters from the surrounding hills. His aides came back with seventy "strapping young men, all in the gorgeous feather headdresses of their tribe and a brand-new coat of red and blue paint." To cover their nakedness, Martin bought the warriors red blankets, which they wore, but "at a rakish angle that made them, as clothing, rather ineffective."

From Meru the Johnsons undertook their most remote safari to date. They passed through plains teeming with game and saw their first oryx, a large black-and-white-faced antelope, and gerenuk, a long-necked antelope with an oddly small head. Shortly into their travels, Martin and Osa saw their first duiker—a small, elusive antelope that normally remains hidden in the cover of forests. Later, when they met an exiled Meru chief along the road, they were reminded of Nagapate. Though Osa thought him "[f]ilthy, hideous of countenance, cruel of expression," she remarked that "he has yet a commanding aspect that no white, educated in the schools of civilization to a realization of his own ultimate powerlessness, could attain." Martin photographed the chief, who had been deposed because he could not accept the "namby-pamby British laws," and his wife. He would not give up his people's warring ways that regarded "fighting and manhood as synonymous."

Quail, grouse, and guinea fowl were everywhere in this country. Osa shot several to make as a gift to their host at Isiolo, the next town on their route. Isiolo was a cattle quarantine station; nomadic Samburu and Boran people herded their cattle through the region, where rinderpest (hoof and mouth disease) killed both cattle and wildlife. It was also a trading post for several tribes who bought and sold weapons, sugar, salt, coffee, and calico on this "highway between the desert and civilization." The station was run by a veterinarian named Macdonough, whom they had contacted to let him know their safari would be coming through. When they arrived, they offered their birds to Macdonough, and they discovered he had gathered several dozen game birds with which to greet them, as well. They laughed at their mutual good-will. He had already set up tents and storehouses for the safari, so they settled in quite easily. Martin and Osa spent Christmas with Macdonough, dining with him and one Lieutenant Douglas. Their meal was a gourmet feast of wild game from the African plains and the finest of English and American "tinned delicacies"—including hominy grits and plum pudding.

The day after Christmas, Major Pedler, the officer in charge of transport for the East African Army, arrived. The major wanted a lion hunt, and the Johnsons, anxious to see more of the great cats, joined him enthusiastically. They rode on mules, searching the landscape for signs of lion. John began to wonder if lions even existed here, as there were so few signs of them. They found nothing that day but tried one last time, for John's sake. When they stopped for lunch in a *donga* (ravine), Macdonough's gun bearer scared up a rhinoceros, which charged toward their picnic. Martin and Osa quickly hopped to their feet and hid behind trees. John tried to do the same, but the rhinoceros caught sight of him and charged. Before anyone could think, the major grabbed his gun and killed the rhino.

Hoping to have a more controlled lion encounter, Martin and Osa decided rather than search for lions, they would lure them with two zebra carcasses as bait. At nightfall, they rode back on the mules. "It was an eery ride," Martin thought. "There was no moon, the night was softly brilliant with the light of the low-hanging tropical stars, but the light was not intense enough to dispel the earth shadows, every one of which seemed to us, as we rode, our nerves strained for animal enemies, to harbor a living thing in its deep blackness. From all sides the noises of the plain beat on our ears. The laughter of the hyenas, which so often, when we were safe in camp, had been contagiously comical, sounded mocking, threatening."

Heading back across the plains, they spotted a line of six lions running single file. "It gave me a strange feeling to see them," said Martin. "When you have lived all your life without seeing wild animals, you get used to thinking of lions and tigers as unrealities, belonging in the same category as witches and ghosts and other childish nightmares. And now here I was, wide-awake, alert, in the full bright light of an equatorial afternoon, watching lions as calmly as if they had been jack-rabbits started from the autumn woods of Kansas."

The men were behind on foot when Ferraragi, who was carrying a gun, as usual, thought he heard a lion. He cocked the gun but then tripped. The bullet ricocheted off the gravel ground, sending pieces flying into the air that lodged into his skin like shrapnel. Macdonough treated Ferraragi's wounds, but the biggest wound was to his ego. Angered that the gun was broken, Martin fired him. Ferraragi moped around in despair. Three days later, Martin hired him back, but with a firm warning to be more careful. They were about to move into the wilderness and could not afford the risk of such careless injuries or broken equipment.

White hunter Andrew Rattray came to Isiolo to fetch supplies and invite the Johnsons to his ranch, seven miles up the Isiolo River. Rattray had three clay houses with grass roofs built on his property, and several paddocks that he was using to domesticate and train Grevy's zebras. "Rattray," Martin said, "is one of the British freelances you are always running into doing strange things in out-of-the-way parts of the world." And indeed, he had trained several zebras to take a harness. They were, he argued, better pack animals for African expeditions as they were immune to tsetse flies, which often felled imported livestock, and they could live off the wild vegetation of the dry plains of Africa.

But Rattray's place offered more than the novelty and intrigue of domesticated zebras—it also had wild cats. Having spotted three lions nearby, Rattray fetched Martin and his cameras. He told several men to get tin pans, with which they would scare the lions toward the camera. When six lions sprang from the bushes, Osa raised her rifle, but Martin told her to wait, hoping they'd come closer. Unfortunately, he didn't have the right lens to capture the moment, and, frustrated, he swore he would not return to Africa without a camera fitted with four lenses at the ready.

Along the Gara Mara River, which "was now nothing but a sun-baked channel" dried by the heat, they looked for lions in the reeds. When Osa thought she saw one, she grabbed her gun. Martin heard a growl, and nine lions soon emerged into the open. Though Martin did not have the camera ready, he looked back at them, thinking how "strangely unterrifying" they were. "They seemed," thought Martin, "like huge, mild dogs." Farther along the dried riverbed, they saw a dead rhinoceros sunken in the mud; it must have drowned there in the middle of the watering hole.

Inspired by these encounters, Osa decided to hunt lion alone, but Rattray refused to allow her to go unescorted. Martin, however, was of a different opinion. "I was for letting her do as she liked," Martin retorted. "I knew her courage to be equal to that of most men." But Rattray insisted, so Martin went along despite Osa's protests. A few men helped them carry their guns and supplies to the blind, set the zebra bait, and then left them alone. They nestled down into the four-foot-deep, seven-foot-wide pit and covered the top with thorny bushes. As the temperature cooled, they pulled blankets around them, listening for the sounds of the African night. It was oddly silent, absent even of the lion roars they wished for, yet feared. Martin wondered if

Osa was still a bit insulted by his presence or whether she was glad to be spending this rare moment alone, away from the rest of their safari companions. Surrounded by people as they constantly were, romance must have been infrequent. They had always, however, been more attracted to each other's gumption than a fantasy of romance.

Though they did not hear her coming, a lioness soon took the bait. Her hands shaking, Osa aimed and shot at the lioness, sending dirt flying down on top of them. The lioness hid behind the zebra kill, seemingly wounded, and cried for an hour before falling silent. They knew they could not emerge to inspect their prize until daylight, so they tried to sleep—Martin more successfully than Osa. In her light doze, she heard sounds outside and awoke to find another lioness at the kill. Osa woke Martin, and he steadied his hand and shot. The lioness fell "without a whimper," but she was not dead. A few minutes later she was looking suspiciously down into the blind.

Martin shot again and the lioness fell dead, but the Johnsons, covered in dirt, could do nothing but sleep and wait. At three o'clock in the morning, Osa watched as a male lion approached the kill. She took aim and waited for a good shot, but the lion suddenly leaped toward the blind, looked in, and then veered away. At last, daylight broke, and Martin and Osa emerged from the pit. The lioness Martin had shot lay where it fell during the night, but Osa's had left a trail of blood leading into the bush. When the men arrived to help them back to camp, the lioness emerged from its cover, angry and injured. It leaped onto the back of one porter, clawing his flesh, then fled into the forest. Martin and Osa dared not go after the angered, injured lioness for fear it would attack one of them.

Back at Rattray's ranch, one day, while they were resting, Rattray arrived on the back of a mule, nearly torn and scratched to death. They sent for Macdonough, who came immediately, but he ultimately sent the patient to the nearest doctor, one hundred miles away, as Rattray's wounds were too severe for him to treat.

Rattray had been hunting when a leopard approached his bait. It was very unusual, he said, for leopards to be about in the middle of the day. He had fired his gun but missed, and the animal leaped at him. The rifle jammed, and he tried to keep her claws away from his face by grabbing her throat. For minutes he held the leopard as the men with him stood stunned. Rattray couldn't find his voice to command them. The leopard clung to him with her claws, he estimated, for fifteen minutes before he lost his grip and let her go, assuming the worst. But instead of doing away with him, the leopard ran off into the bush. Rattray was the worse for wear, though. He was in pain for six months afterward, and it was a full year before he could resume his zebra-training project.

Angered by the event, Macdonough, Lieutenant Douglas, Cotter, Osa, and Martin went to track down the leopard that had nearly killed their friend, taking Rattray's dog along with them. The dog recognized the scent and alerted the party, but the leopard sprung at the dog, breaking its leg. As the leopard leaped, however, someone's shot had struck home, and it was killed. "She was the only animal," declared Martin, "that I ever saw die without regret." He considered it a rogue example of the species.

Rattray was skeptical about their unmapped lake and told the Johnsons they ought to go to some water holes in the nearby Chobe Hills instead. The water holes were currently filled with giraffes, Grevy's zebras, and rhinoceroses. While the lake expedition was uncertain, he knew they would get good footage of wildlife amid the beautiful scenery at Chobe, so they decided to go to there for a few weeks. Though it was just a few miles from Rattray's, the journey there was one they would never forget.

As they walked, they came across a lava field that stretched as far as the eye could see. Dried lava lay in flat stretches, broken by chunks that made the terrain uneven. Martin suggested they go another way, but the men wanted to go across the lava because it was the shortest route to the hills. Because the surface of the lava was hot from the sun, they waited until sundown before setting

Osa holds the hurt paw of Rattray's dog beside the leopard that attacked his master.

out. The barefoot porters seemed unfazed at first by the rough surface, singing as they walked, but soon the terrain caused painful sores on their feet, and they stopped after fifteen miles.

In the morning, the lava was once again "blistering hot." Osa felt so worn out and frightened; this experience reminded her of being forced up the mountain by Nagapate's people. "My skin burned, my eyeballs ached, and there was a drum-like pounding in my head," she remembered. Her boots were torn by the course, dried lava. Martin's were, too, but he was too worried about his cameras and film, which were far behind them with the porters, to notice. The porters, slowed down by their painful feet, had also failed to fill their own canteens, and they would die in the heat if they fell too far behind—but they could not make it across the lava fields with their loads. In late afternoon, Jerramani allowed them to leave their packs so they could at least get to safety. Within an hour, they were safely across the lava field, which emptied onto sand that stung the abrasions on the porters' feet.

Martin took a few of the healthier men to search for water, telling Osa to listen for three shots as a sign he had found some. Jerramani set up Osa's cot, and she dozed to the sound of men moaning, lions roaring, and what she thought was a leopard coughing with pain. She must have fallen into a deep sleep as she missed Martin's signal. The men woke her up and began running toward the sound of his shots. Osa followed to find Martin smiling but weary. They set up camp by the water and sent some of the men back for the abandoned supplies, while the others nursed their feet in the water. When the camera equipment arrived, Martin anxiously checked it all and, to his relief, found that it was fine. Osa knew he was more tired than he seemed, so she forced him into bed, even though it was the middle of the day. When she took off his boots, his feet were bleeding. As she and Aloni washed them, he deliriously mumbled how wonderful he felt, then slept for twenty-four hours.

After this difficult start, Martin and Osa began to enjoy themselves. Camp was restful, and 'Mpishi's full breakfasts of eggs, meat, toast, and coffee gave them the strength to work in the field all day. Osa enjoyed fishing in the Guaso Nyiro River, and hunting and providing food for the table, considering it her "wifely duty." She enjoyed the routine of camp life, organizing and dividing the labor, planning menus, and helping 'Mpishi prepare the meals. She bathed every day in the canvas tub and dressed for dinner. "I made it an invariable rule to keep my hair well brushed and arranged," she advised, "and to give as much attention to manicure and beauty treatments as though we were in the heart of New York rather than in the depths of so-called darkest Africa. It always seemed to me that I owed it to Martin to look my very best no matter what the circumstances." The only comforts she missed were the fresh fruits and vegetables from her garden.

Just two hours from camp, there were five water holes in a two-mile-long chain. Animals of all kinds came there in droves. The men built several blinds of stone and thorny bushes—one on each side of each hole so the direction of the wind would not affect filming. In order to avoid scaring wildlife away, they had to enter the blinds before sunrise. Osa enjoyed the early-morning walks along trails, beaten down by rhinos, that wound through the lush forested hills. In the still-dark morning, she noticed the soft sweet scent of the foliage and the fresh feel of the air. "All about us were the waking sounds of the wilderness," she gushed, "birds chirping, zebra barking, lions exploiting their deepest bass notes, and rhino crashing, with angry snorts, through the underbrush."

Martin and Osa remained in the blinds all day, sometimes separating into different blinds to double their luck. Zebras, gazelles, giraffes, ostriches, rhinoceroses, and buffaloes came down from the hills to drink in the morning, three to four hundred of them all drinking peacefully together. "We were amazed at the extent to which they respected one another's rights," remarked Osa. "I never did get over a sort of Noah's Ark unreality about the whole thing." They took thousands of feet of film before the herds thinned at the sound of an approaching hunting party.

When they were ready to leave, they knew they had to do something to protect the porters' feet from the scars of the lava field. Martin and Osa went out to hunt a buffalo so they could make sandals from the hide, but as they were searching the swamp, they found not a buffalo, but a rhinoceros. Martin quickly set up his camera and stationed Osa at the crank while he approached. Osa watched his excitement. He was shaking, his eyes wide, and his jaw firm with determination. He shouted. The rhino charged rather lazily, then looked at Martin, confused. The animal seemed to be mulling over its next move. Then, having made up its mind, it snorted and ran directly toward them. Martin shot but only wounded it. The sound of the gun, however, sent all the other animals running from the donga. Zebras, oryx, and buffaloes went charging past them so close and so quickly, the Johnsons could not move. They waved their arms and yelled to make sure the herds went around—and not through—them, but the buffaloes did not flinch. Martin and Osa took up their guns and shot in the air until the herd divided around them. They escaped with wounds only from the rocks flying up from stampeding hooves.

Farther north, rhinoceroses were everywhere, and the Johnsons got plenty of pictures of, in Osa's opinion, "the ugly and unpredictable beasts." "The rhino seems old from the time he is born," decided Martin, "old and overfed and stupid and bad-tempered. . . . He wanders about alone or with one companion. He is too disagreeable for society." One rhinoceros stood perfectly posed, and Martin told Osa to man the camera while he instigated a charge. Another rhinoceros appeared from behind a rock, and both came directly at Martin. He redirected them to run past the camera, but Osa was so shaken with fear that she failed to crank the camera. Martin reminded her of their tasks: "I'll get the action; you get the picture, and don't you worry about me."

They set up camp in a grove of ivory-nut trees and spent ten days sitting in blinds photographing oryx and reticulated giraffes, the most common of the nine giraffe subspecies. Martin thought this the most comfortable camp so far. "Though we spent our lives in wandering," Martin explained, "Osa and I are really the most domestic couple you can imagine. The only difference between us and millions of other home-loving folk is that we make our home on the go." Martin set up his typewriter and wrote letters while 'Mpishi's fresh bread baked in the oven.

Osa delighted in the rest and took up her rod to catch dinner in the Guaso Nyiro River. As she walked back into camp, Martin watched and thought that in her safari outfit she looked "like a sturdy Boy Scout, trudging along in her khaki 'shorts' and shirt, her broad-brimmed double terai hat held under the chin by an elastic, her golf-stockings, and her stout mannish boots." Osa, Martin explained, "is a pretty woman" who looks wonderful in "the fuss and frippery of New York. But," he continued, "I think her prettiest and I like best to see her in her wilderness wardrobe." Not aware of his thoughtful gaze, Osa approached Martin

Fishing was among Osa's greatest pleasures on safari and she made it her wifely duty to hunt, gather, and prepare meals for Martin while on expedition.

with news. It wasn't just the two hundred pounds of fish she had caught that sparked her excitement; at the river, she had seen a hippopotamus.

Martin didn't quite share her enthusiasm. He knew hippopotamuses were too difficult to photograph, especially when submerged in water, so he went to look for rhinos instead. They had learned some important techniques from filming rhinos. When filming them on the open plains, they didn't have the benefit of a blind to shield them. They had to find the rhino, set up the equipment without scaring it away, and then carefully begin cranking the camera. Osa would then shoot her gun to get its attention. At the noise, the rhinoceros usually turned and sometimes began to charge, but it was usually a bluff charge meant to scare the adversary away. Martin and Osa discovered that if they stood their ground, they could get good footage of rhinos and be in no danger—most of the time.

This did not abate Osa's fears or hatred for the creatures. Once, when she was supposed to be filming two rhinos that turned to threaten them, she abandoned the camera and took up her gun instead. Martin was severely disappointed to miss such action and did not hide his feelings. Osa, in turn, cried on the way back to camp. Martin tried to comfort her but was firm in his resolve to never stop filming, no matter the circumstances. They made a pact that in the future, "whichever of us was at the camera would stick to the camera no matter what happened, until it became apparent that either the picture or the life of one of us must be sacrificed."

Martin was beginning to respect Osa's daring, however. "[F]or bravery and steadiness and endurance Osa is the equal of any man I ever saw," he proclaimed, "as a comrade in the wilderness she is better than any man I ever saw." Rhinos, however, were her Achilles heel. "She does not like rhinos," Martin explained. "When she has nightmares, safe in our New York apartment, it is rhinos she sees coming up the fire-escape. But any one who has ever met a rhino at close quarters will excuse her. Nobody loves a rhino."

When they moved on from the Chobe Hills, they traversed a desert landscape to Archer's Post—a place Martin thought rather depressing. It consisted of nothing but a few grass huts on top of "the most barren hill on earth" with the dry riverbed of the Guaso Nyiro below. A rotund, Swahili police officer, Mohammed Sudan, was in charge and supervised nearly everything in the town, which was primarily a camel trading post. Archer's Post made the whole desert look dreary, in Martin's opinion, while "[u]ninhabited desert never seems dreary to me." The desert, he concluded, was not for settlement but for wandering through.

Osa and Martin camped below the barren hill along the river, where trees provided some shade in the harsh landscape. Two Indian dukas stood across the way from them. It was odd to see the river so dry there, as it was a rushing stream of rapids and waterfalls just one mile away. In the morning, they heard word of a rhinoceros about five miles from the post and set out to get pictures, as Martin did not think they had enough. "It was blazing hot," said Martin as they set out across the desert. "After we left the river, the country was parched desert that reflected the heat and intensified it many fold." They had walked for about eight miles when their guide told them he was lost. Stopping to eat lunch at an old lake bed, Osa spotted a rhino just across from where they sat. Martin was excited to get these pictures until he returned to the post to hear three, including an infant, had come right through their camp.

Martin still hadn't had his fill of rhinos, but Osa certainly had. To avoid going on another hunt, Martin said, "she became very domestic, and found something to do near camp." When Martin returned from his search, he saw a note Osa had left, telling him she had killed a greater kudu, one of the rarest of African animals. Despite his growing distaste for hunting, Martin was excited to have it "for our collection of trophies." He went to meet her to help bring the kudu home, but it turned out to be a waterbuck. Osa had quite a day of collecting, however, returning to camp with a small crocodile, fish, fowl, and a caged butterfly with eight-inch wings.

Martin and Osa had plenty of time to spare while they waited at Archer's Post for their porters to arrive from Meru, so Martin, Jerramani, and twenty of their men went to explore the Chobe Hills again. They avoided most of the lava beds this time but were ruthlessly bitten by spirillum ticks. They were lucky that these particular spirillum ticks were not disease carriers, as an infection from one could bring on intense fever, paralysis, or even death. Back at Archer's Post, they saw many safaris come through, including that of the Duke of Orleans (heir to the French throne), who was collecting for a scientific society, and that of Major Dugmore, who, like Martin, was famous for hunting with a camera instead of a gun.

Finally, the porters reached Archer's Post, and the Johnsons began preparing for the final leg of their journey. Martin's father,

John, would stay behind as planned and meet them on their way back. Though this promised to be the roughest of their safaris, Martin was excited to enter "the quiet, clean, far places where not even the remotest echoes of a noisy industrial world could be heard." "When we left Archer's Post," he wrote, "our last contact with civilization was broken."

Martin and Osa set out in their Fords to the northern Kenyan town of Marsabit. They drove 245 miles across the Kaisoot Desert—a "succession of burning days," Martin complained. But the cool, star-filled nights nearly made up for the heat. They stopped at a place known as "the Wells," which was nothing but three small wells dug into the dry riverbed. From there they went to Karo, passing their porters, who had left two days before them. Karo was less impressive than the Wells. It was "just a name situated on the brink of a dry river." They dug for water, but it took until morning before they coaxed enough to fill their canteens. They waited for the porters there and watched giraffes, zebras, oryx, gerenuks, cheetahs, and rhinos. After Karo, the roads became more rough; they were nothing more than narrow caravan routes interrupted by boulders and sand pits. The heavy cars sunk in the soft sand, and several times they had to push and carry the cars. Needless to say, progress was slow.

When they reached the Merille River at Longai, they found it just as dry as the others. Up the valley, however, Martin and Osa found a water hole scenically surrounded by red rocks that "looked for all the world like a miniature Grand Canyon." Martin had his men build a blind in the side of the steep rocks, where he and Osa slept so they could awake early to film wildlife. The night sounds were only of hyenas at first, which they found more comical than terrifying. But later in the night, Osa awoke to lions roaring in the distance. She sat up until the sound died down, keeping Martin awake, as well. They had both fallen asleep when Osa heard two rhinoceros fighting outside the blind. She poked Martin in the ribs to get his attention. When the rhinos stopped butting horns, they moved out of sight, and shortly thereafter rocks came sliding down the slope right past the Johnsons' blind. When they looked out, there were ten rhinoceroses in sight, all staging their own battles. At dawn, they disappeared into the bush.

In the morning, Martin walked into the valley to look for elephants. He jumped from rock to rock, making his way down, when he saw "a flash of yellow" beneath him. "Lions!" He held back a moment, realizing it was not lions but hyenas, who withdrew into a cave. "The feeling of not knowing what is going to show up next is one of the fascinations of Africa," enthused Martin. "You go along, fearing to see a dangerous beast, yet expectantly on the lookout. Every noise is alarming and exciting. The most innocent landscape takes on an air of mystery; that heap of rocks may harbor a lion, that thicket an elephant."

The following night, Martin stayed in the blind alone, as Osa once again swore off seeing any more rhinoceroses. It seemed, however, there was no escape in these wilds. In the middle of the night, she arrived at the blind, telling Martin a rhino had come right into their camp. She figured she may as well be with him if rhinos were following her around anyway. The night was filled with animal sounds, but they spotted none.

At their next camp, in Longania, hyenas stole meat drying right next to the fire. They were so brazen, one dragged a meat strip directly over Zabenelli's face. He awoke, panicked to think a lion was dragging him away. The other men made a big joke of the episode and mockingly called him Simba for days. Jerramani mimicked a lion roar every time he saw him.

They began to travel by moonlight, first to Lasamis, then to Marsabit. The road to Marsabit was a packed-down caravan trail that made travel somewhat swifter. Near noon, however, they came across rocky forests that slowed them down considerably. They unloaded the cars so the men could carry them over impassable rocks, then reloaded the cars on the other side. They did this several times, painfully slowing their progress, but Martin and Osa did not give up. "Few things are impossible," Martin said, sounding almost like his mentor, Jack London, "when you are faced with the necessity of accomplishing them."

Soon they saw the peak of Mount Marsabit—an extinct volcano—that rose abruptly from the flat desert to 5,600 feet above sea level. The town of Marsabit sat on the side of the mountain. Martin and Osa felt the change in landscape as they left the desert for the forest. Trees tangled with vines, creepers, and moss towered over them. Hundreds of thousands of butterflies "of every conceivable color" swarmed around them. Martin left Osa and the men to set up camp while he searched for water. He found only a mere trickle of a stream before darkness fell, but then he could not find his way back to the camp. "The forest that had seemed, in the sunlight, uninhabited, was now peopled with all sorts of animals," said Martin, "real and imaginary." When he didn't return, Osa set off a radium flare, which gave Martin a glowing sign of direction.

Finding this forest alluring, Martin and Osa decided to stay and explore before going any farther. There they met Boran herdsmen and their women, whose bobbed hairstyles Osa admired. The blunt cut of the style reminded her of drawings of ancient Egyptians. One day they found four rhinoceroses. Osa complained of a blister and went back to camp, where she watched Kalowatt interact with curious baboons. The ape called to them from a rock, but every time they crept forward, Kalowatt fearfully ran away.

The Johnsons stayed at this camp for three weeks, establishing a regular schedule of morning walks along game trails that led to a crater. They saw many buffaloes and rhinoceroses, and hopeful signs of elephant activity. Martin, unfortunately, had to shoot one rhino that charged toward him. Though he regretted the kill, it seemed it was either the rhino or himself. If a rhinoceros attacks a human, it gores with its teeth, and this can lead to a gruesome and painful death. Martin did not wish to take the chance. Still, Martin reflected, of the 120 rhinoceroses he had taken photos of, they had only killed four. That seemed a fairly good record for their work—and for the rhinos, which proved not nearly as ferocious as their reputation.

When they broke camp, they moved on to the town of Marsabit, where they met an elephant tracker named Boculy (Martin's accounts call him Boguni). Both Martin and Osa found him a little odd. "There was something uncanny about [him]," Martin thought. "I do not know how old he was, but he had the air of having lived forever and having been born old." Osa saw in him a "little, wizened old man with sore eyes and a jaw that was curiously lopsided, he seemed to appear out of nowhere and, presenting himself to Martin, signified his wish to join our safari." Despite his oddity, they took to him immediately and soon learned they could not have done so well without him. "There was," she continued, "a curious dignity about him, a sureness that we needed him more than he needed us. We engaged him on the spot."

However uncanny Boculy appeared to the Johnsons, Martin later learned he was a rather powerful man among his people. He owned 250 camels, spoke most of the languages of the plains and desert tribes, and had connections among them that granted favors everywhere he traveled. Martin completely trusted his tracking skills: "If Boculy told me I'd find elephants in front of the N.Y. Public Library, I'd believe him. . . ."

Osa tried to treat Boculy's sore eyes, but nothing seemed to work. Every couple of days, his eyesight suffered. His crooked jaw, which got in his way when he ate and when he talked, was the result of what Osa called "a fantastic tale of an encounter with an equally fantastic elephant," which the Johnsons at first did not believe. Martin revealed more details of the supposed encounter but still expressed doubt about its veracity. "He said that the break was the result of an encounter with an elephant on Mount Kilimanjaro," explained Martin. "I believed that, but I found it hard to credit [Boculy's] story of how the elephant bore down upon him, brandishing in his trunk an uprooted tree that he used as a club."

Boculy impressed Osa and Martin with his intimate knowledge of the African wilderness.

Osa and Martin followed Boculy even though it seemed he was breaking the cardinal rule of tracking wildlife by approaching them upwind, they found he had a more intimate knowledge than any guide they had previously employed. Part of Boculy's gift was a superior understanding of the winds. He knew that in this area the winds blew in currents. "[Boculy] knew those currents as a sailor knows the currents of the sea," admired Martin, "and he could get nearer to an elephant without being discovered than any one else I have ever met." Boculy "had wisdom concerning elephants that went beyond mere knowledge," reported Osa. In fact, the other natives called him "Little Brother of the Elephants."

Boculy certainly knew the region, so they asked him about Percival's unmapped lake. He seemed to know of something but did not offer to take them there immediately. After that Boculy was gone for several days, and Martin and Osa set out from Marsabit to look for the lake. A few days later Boculy found them; he had news of elephants nearby. For days they trekked through forests, climbing rugged trails, not knowing where they were being led. Finally they reached the top of a cliff and, looking down, saw a beautiful lake. Boculy looked at them knowingly, rubbing his head and stomach, as he had a habit of doing. This was, he indicated, the lake for which they had been searching. He had known it all along but had not wanted to share its location until he knew they were trustworthy. After a few days watching them work—with cameras and not with guns—Boculy seemed satisfied they would not disturb this sanctuary.

The unmapped lake was a water-filled crater shaped like a spoon, lying a quarter mile wide and three-quarters of a mile long. Water vines and blue lilies sprouted from the water and surrounded its edge. Lava rocks lined the shore all the way to the forest, which stretched beyond on all sides. More wildlife than they could count drank from the shores, while egrets, ducks, and cranes hovered above. "It's paradise, Martin!" Osa declared.

So as not to disturb the wildlife, Martin and Osa set up camp six miles away, on the border of forest and plains. They rested while the men set up the tents, erected grass huts, and carefully laid a ring of thornbushes around the camp perimeter. Martin and Osa experienced a quiet calm in having finally found their longed-for destination.

Boculy claimed there were twenty-five thousand elephants near this lake, which they now dubbed Lake Paradise. Martin thought this figure sounded like "a gross exaggeration," but after hearing the sounds in the forest that first night, he changed his mind. "I would have accepted without challenge an estimate of a hundred thousand," he declared. It was the noisiest night they had ever experienced, signaling the abundance of wildlife. At dawn, it ended in "a crescendo of animal and bird calls." The noise elephants made in the forest was forbidding, sounding to Martin like they were destroying every tree in their path—and then some. "The great beasts are like children that want to see what makes the wheels go 'round," he said, "whatever they do not understand they investigate by destroying it." But Boculy was unafraid. The noise, he explained, was merely elephants feeding from the tender shoots at the tops of the trees, which required them to bend or break the lower branches to reach.

At breakfast that first morning, three elephants strolled lazily within sight, throwing dust over their backs and "just enjoying the sun and the air." The Johnsons delighted in their casual airs. "Why this place is their home," Martin said, amazed, "and they've let us move right in!" They walked back to the lake, where Martin set up his camera. He was getting wonderful footage of elephants mingling peacefully when he told Osa to walk into the picture. As she got nearer, she began to think of the wild elephants as circus animals and imagined it safe to "go right up and feed them and pat their wrinkled trunks. To walk toward them seemed the most natural thing in the world to do. I even decided the big one's name was Jumbo . . . it hadn't occurred to me to be afraid." But when she got too close to the animals, she startled them. She froze for a second, stunned at the wheeling elephants, who now seemed more wild than a circus act. They began to run away, but Osa, instead of doing the same herself, started to chase after them. "It was a ludicrous sight," remembered Martin, "that tiny, khaki-clad figure, in pursuit of those great hulks." Osa heard his "roar of laughter" and turned back. "What would you have done if you'd caught them?" he teased. Gathering up what remained of her dignity and feeling quite silly, she replied, "I had to show them they couldn't bluff me."

The scene ruined for filming, they decided to move on. Boculy led them along a game trail to a watering hole surrounded by trees draped in silver moss. Two elephants stood in the pool, leisurely swinging their trunks and fanning their ears. Colorful butterflies danced around the elephants and lilies in the pool. "We gazed in breathless bewilderment," said Martin. "The whole picture seemed fantastically unreal." Martin took out his camera and took pictures of the scene, but, as they discovered on their

When filming approaching wildlife, Osa stood ahead of the camera with gun ready.

twenty-five-mile trek around the lake that day, this was just normal life at Lake Paradise. The lake was surrounded by water holes frequented by elephants.

For three months they explored the lake from their nearby camp, observing the elephants each day and so often that many became familiar, and the Johnsons could distinguish individuals. Martin and Osa began to learn the pleasures of watching a single elephant for hours as it ate, slept, snacked, and slept again. "They seemed so wise and so gentle," mused Martin, and "unsuspicious." The lack of large tuskers implied the herds had indeed been hunted by ivory poachers, but they did not seem afraid of humans. "[T]hey had not known the constant terrifying pursuit that is the lot of animals near the haunts of civilization," theorized Martin. They had been pushed to this remote locale by settlers who drove out the large, destructive creatures of Africa—elephants, rhinos, and hippos—in order to save their crops.

There was at least one tusked bull in the area, and when Martin saw him, he forgot his hatred for hunting and was filled with the desire to make a trophy of the magnificent specimen. Martin took his gun and gave Osa the camera, surrendering to "my man's power over the brute world." He aimed and shot at the elephant's ear, where he had been told the heart lay, but the tusker charged, followed by the six other elephants in view and several more the Johnsons had not seen. Martin shot again, then ran toward Osa, reloading his gun while he did so. He turned and fired yet again, but the elephants were nearly on top of him, so he kept running. Osa loyally kept cranking the camera until the very last minute, when she reached for her gun, fired, and watched as the elephant fell nearly on top of the camera. The herd scattered, and Martin collapsed in exhaustion. Jerramani rallied the men, who carried Osa back to camp on their shoulders as they sang with delight: "Memsahib has killed an elephant."

Martin and Osa's three months at this camp taught them the country and, with Boculy's help, the behavior of elephants. They explored along ancient elephant trails, some hundreds of years old, laid down as orderly as city streets through the forest. Trails led the Johnsons, and the elephants, to the lake, to feeding grounds, to the desert, to the plain, and to water holes. During the rains, the elephants left Lake Paradise and stayed on the dried desert and plains until they ended. In the heat, they remained in the shade and cool waters of the lake. What knowledge—and pictures—could they gain by staying even longer at this remote location? Martin began to conceive of a plan to make a film portraying the entire life cycle of a wild elephant. Even after they left Lake Paradise, Martin and Osa felt the strong urge to return.

When they were back in Nairobi, they showed Percival their photographs and moving pictures. He approved, Osa said, "with the usual restraint of the Britisher," but his enthusiasm to see Lake Paradise was apparent. "I doubt that even a score of wild horses," he said, "could keep me from joining you on your next trip."

———◆———

"Mr. And Mrs. Martin Johnson are the latest tripod nimrods to return to Broadway with the pelts and carcasses (in celluloid) of giraffes and jungle tigers," announced *Time* magazine in late May of 1923. Their feature film documenting the wildlife of Africa, *Trailing African Wild Animals,* exposed—in slick advertising copy of the day—the "mighty monarchs of the murky morass." Martin and writer Terry Ramsaye edited the film to create the most excitement for audiences through close animal encounters. Ramsaye wrote the titles for the silent feature, which followed the Johnsons' search for Lake Paradise, and the titles emphasized that the Johnsons only shot in situations of extreme danger. The Johnsons had achieved something other filmmakers had not. They had made an entirely authentic film of animals that seemed, continued the reviewer for *Time,* "uncommonly realistic." Though the reviewer admitted to knowing African wildlife only through zoo visits, he knew the film was truthful, he indicated, because it was chosen for the archives of the American Museum of Natural History.

Osa emerged an even bigger star from this film. "Her distinctly feminine personality," wrote another reviewer in the *New York World,* "forms a striking contrast with the barbaric and quite evidently dangerous surroundings." She was praised not only for her daring, but for adding to the film's "attractiveness." As a result of the film, Osa was featured in an advertisement for Ford motorcars—the brand they had used on the expedition. The magazine ad printed a photograph of a young and enthusiastic Osa leaning on one of their Fords. The copy called her "a brave little lady" and "intrepid," repeating her supposed claim that their Fords were "the biggest aid in exploring darkest Africa." For his part, Martin published an article in *Asia* magazine about their trials and tribulations hunting animals with a camera. However, the best publicity to come from this film by far was the association with the American Museum of Natural History.

Martin went to the famed New York City institution to meet Carl Akeley, who had first suggested he take his cameras to Africa. At the time, Akeley was working on a bronze sculpture of a native African lion hunt. He asked Martin how his representation of the Nandi tribesman looked. Was it true to life? The two were on a first-name basis within a few hours, and Martin began to visit the museum several times a week to talk with Akeley. He watched him work on his series of bronze lion scenes and listened to his stories about Africa and his plans for a hall of African animals at the museum. His ideas for the hall were still developing, and Martin said he did a lot of "thinking out loud." Martin invited Akeley to dinner at their apartment, and he came several times, delighted with the young adventuring couple and with their pet Kalowatt.

Akeley praised Martin's films to museum colleagues, declaring that his work presented a truthful glimpse of Africa. "[I]t is absolutely free from any form of fake, misrepresentation or disagreeable feature of killing or torturing animals," Akeley asserted; it is "a real Natural History production with no 'bunk' of any sort, chock full of beauty and thrills." Martin wrote to the director of the American Museum of Natural History, Daniel E. Pomeroy, outlining his plans for another African expedition. He said he planned to create several films from this next safari. One would show native life at Meru "on the order of Nanook of the North"— a narrative documentary of Inuk life, filmed in 1922 by Robert J. Flaherty and considered both an accurate portrayal of native life and a drama entertaining enough to draw popular audiences that Martin apparently found quite inspirational as a model. The other films would feature wildlife and would be drawn from footage at Lake Paradise and the Congo, with a small film on baby animals to draw the interest of children and families. "[E]very picture," professed Martin, "will be an authentic record of the animals, natives and the country." Martin suggested he would stay in the field and send the films back to a production company for editing and release.

Pomeroy was impressed with *Trailing African Wild Animals* and was anxious for the young photographer to go back to Africa. He helped Martin establish a corporation to fund another expedition along the lines described in his letter, with the museum donating $150,000. There was one stipulation—that they include a film featuring the native lion-spearing hunt, with which Akeley was so fascinated.

With this support behind him, Martin sought the sponsorship of photography's most prominent name—George Eastman. Martin and Osa made a trip to Rochester to meet with Eastman and, after a bungled first meeting, returned to present their pitch more confidently. Martin followed up with a letter. "As I told you in Rochester," he said, appealing to Eastman's conservation sense, "the game of Africa is doomed. . . Unless the animals of Africa are photographed now it will never be done, and I am egotistical enough to think I am the only one with sufficient tropical training in this sort of work, to do it right . . . we must not let the Big Game of Africa become extinct without this permanent record which I plan to make."

Akeley also wrote to Eastman, showing his support for Martin's work and telling him how Martin's expedition would assist in collecting and making images for his hall of African wildlife. Motion pictures were important to "scientific and educational" endeavors, he argued, representing "life histories of wild animals." Martin, claimed Akeley, "has no superior in wild life cinematography." He knew the technology and the lighting, and he had the endurance to work in the harsh environments of Africa. "It seems to us that he has all of the necessary equipment," Akeley concluded, "including a partner, Mrs. Johnson, who is everything that a partner in such an undertaking should be." Eastman agreed, and on July 31, 1923, Martin wrote Eastman, thanking him for his support in subscribing to "our African work." "[A]t the end of five years," he promised, "we hope to personally show you the most wonderful film ever made, and prove that your confidence has not been misplaced."

With support for their next expedition secured, Martin and Osa made one last stop in Kansas to visit with their families after a two-year absence. After the buzz of New York City, they found the relaxing pace of home refreshing. Osa fished every day and, though she didn't catch anything, enjoyed sitting and being outdoors. Kalowatt and Martin indulged in summer watermelons—and playing in the watermelon patches. But all was not idyllic in Kansas at the time. Martin wrote to Akeley about a Ku Klux Klan march through Chanute, during which five thousand members rallied in white robes with blazing crosses. "I do not like the way they looked in my direction as they marched past," Martin told Akeley, perhaps wondering if he was a target because of his work representing African life. Americans, he thought, did not understand African cultures, and many did not get to know dark-skinned people as he had. Now that he was associated with one of the leading scientific and educational museums in the nation, Martin felt more determined than ever to bring audiences truthful images of African lives.

CHAPTER 4

Living in Paradise

This is certainly Paradise. It must be the most interesting place on earth. No one ever had such a wonderful home.

— Martin Johnson

It would be hard to leave this beautiful wilderness, and I said a little prayer that this spot might be kept as it was, to remain a sanctuary for the animals who loved it.

— Osa Johnson

On December 1, 1923, Martin and Osa said good-bye to friends and family on the docks in New York. Osa's parents and grandmother had come from Kansas, as well as Martin's father and sister, Freda. Their new friends and supporters Dan Pomeroy and George Eastman were also there. Watching her family shrink into specks in the distance as the boat left the harbor drove Osa to tears, thinking of the four-year journey they were about to begin and how much she would miss everyone. Her tears annoyed Martin. Things were better than ever, he told her. "[W]hat more do you want?" he asked. "My husband went right on, piling up such a weight of masculine logic against my wholly feminine, illogical tears that I should have been crushed with humiliation," said Osa. Martin's rant came from his fear that she would grow tired of their expeditions and go home to Kansas. He hated the thought of losing her because of his chosen lifestyle, worrying that she would "get tired of living the way we do among wild people, wild animals— no home. It's tough on a woman—it must be." When he told her this, Osa replied indignantly, "Why, that's the silliest thing I ever heard," and she determined not to grow sentimental around him again. Despite occasional bouts of homesickness, she too had chosen this life of adventure.

When they arrived in Mombasa nearly two months after leaving New York, they were pleased to see their old cook, 'Mpishi, waving to them from the harbor. After organizing their luggage and supply crates—more than 250 of them—they boarded the railway to Nairobi. This massive number of crates slowed them down considerably, and though they knew the rains were coming, they could do nothing to pick up the pace. Once the rains began, the trip would be impossible. The Guaso Nyiro River would flood, leaving no way across with their supplies. They moved as quickly as they could to Nairobi.

Martin and Osa spent five weeks in Nairobi organizing their trip. All their equipment and supplies had to be repackaged into sixty-pound loads, for the porters would carry nothing heavier. They had eighteen guns, tons of ammunition, twenty-one cameras, photo supplies, water tanks, food, medicine, and clothing. All of this was to be carried by six Willys-Knight safari cars, four motor trucks, five mule wagons, four oxcarts, and two hundred porters.

At the Guaso Nyiro River, Blayney Percival, now retired from his post as game warden, joined their safari, and they began moving, once again, toward Lake Paradise. The now-familiar unmapped lake was Martin and Osa's primary destination, and they planned to stay there for four years, filming and living with the wildlife. Anxious to arrive, Martin suggested a shortcut through the mountains to Archer's Post, but it didn't work. The entire party turned back, having lost sixty-five miles. When the porters began to fall sick with an illness no one recognized, and no medicine in their supplies seemed to help, Osa and Martin sent some of the sick men to Meru by oxcart. Twenty other porters deserted. When they reached Archer's Post, Percival helped reorganize the broken safari, and in two days they were on their way through the Kaisoot Desert, which looked like "a gray, sleepy sea" under cloudy skies. Rain began to fall, making traveling more difficult. The vehicles "bogged repeatedly," forcing them to unload supplies and push and carry the cars over muddy stretches of land.

Their elephant tracker, Boculy, joined them at Kampia Tembo, which was, according to Osa, "a godforsaken government station" of mud huts and unhealthy cattle. The Johnsons were glad to reunite with Boculy, however, and he lifted the whole safari's spirits. What's more, the tracker knew of a shorter route to Lake Paradise. Though skeptical after their last bungled shortcut, they hoped he was right. Boculy led them through the forest with fifty men in front to cut a trail. Osa felt as though they were "creeping through high, tough grass, crashing down ravines, and straining up steep grades." They traveled for ten days through an unfamiliar landscape that seemed to be growing increasingly rough, but Boculy urged them on cheerfully, confident in his route.

Then, on April 12, 1924, they arrived. Lake Paradise was just as enchanting as it had been before. Blue water lilies lay upon its surface, and butterflies, herons, egrets, ducks, cranes, and storks flew overhead. Olive and mahogany trees grew all around. Osa felt a lump in her throat as she imagined "this moment was the fulfillment of one dream and the beginning of another." An elephant that had been serenely bathing in the waters made his way into the forest with a blue water lily wrapped around his tail. Percival held

Osa joins the men pulling their automobile through a rugged donga. Cars made safari easier, but they were not without their limitations.

back tears. "[T]his is rather more astonishing than I had expected it to be," he said, staring with wonder at this hidden sanctuary.

But not all was paradise. Just two hours after their arrival, the rains began, coming down in torrents like they had never seen before. "Unexpected difficulties," confided Osa, "are at once the challenge and the charm of the lives of all explorers." They set up their tents, but "no canvas that was ever made could keep out the water that poured upon us as if tipped from the shore of some celestial sea." The porters and assistants had no shelter at all. Osa tried to appease them with sugar and coffee, and by keeping the fires going.

Between the raindrops, Martin, Percival, and their men erected buildings that would serve them for four years—huts for the men, a house for the Johnsons, guesthouses, and a laboratory. First they worked on a house for their electric-light plant. Though they were worried their batteries had gone bad, it lit up perfectly when it was all put together. Martin and the men then began raising the other buildings, fashioning huts of vertical logs "in African native fashion" covered with a mud and dung mixture that became hard as concrete, then using another mixture of clay and dung to plaster the walls. Dried grass served as roofs. Osa thought the adobe color of the plastered walls and the yellow of the roofs "was very attractive against the pale and darker mahogany greens of the forest."

While Martin was busy building, Osa planted her garden. She had brought seeds and bulbs with her—"enough surplus to start most of the waterholes blooming with flowers"—and was anxious to get them in the soil. Martin and Percival looked skeptically upon her project of planting a garden in the midst of such wildness, thinking the seeds would rot or be eaten by birds. Her garden did succeed, however, yielding beans, peas, sweet corn, turnips, squash, carrots, potatoes, cucumbers, and salsify, as well as cantaloupe and watermelon. Osa was proud to disprove the men's "pessimistic predictions." Even though he had been equally doubtful, Martin advised Percival, "Never argue with a woman. Nine times out of every ten she's right."

Osa also learned about the wild food of the forest, where asparagus, spinach, berries, mushrooms, and wild plums grew. "I think," she pondered, "I relished even more the wild delicacies." Sometimes Osa took watercress seeds with her to water holes, where she planted a few for the elephants—they loved the leafy greens. The abundance of good food and fresh fruit in the forest put the idea of "darkest Africa" out of the Johnsons' minds and proved the myths untrue—at least, not at Lake Paradise.

It was not long before they fell into a neat routine. Each morning, Martin went to the field to take pictures, and each afternoon, he wrote in his diary (though he hated the task). During the rains, Martin and Osa camped in blinds on the desert and plain. Dry season had them looking for wildlife at water holes and in forests.

Martin's photographic equipment was now state-of-the-art and included several specially ordered lenses of all types. Of the five film cameras designed by Carl Akeley, a pair were "mounted

At Lake Paradise, Osa enjoyed the comforts of home in the midst of wild Africa. Here she offers a homemade coconut cake to two Songa men.

together, one taking regularly timed pictures while the other took the same action in slow motion." Akeley designed this specifically for the challenges of filming wildlife. Another of his cameras had four lenses attached for instant distance adjustments. Martin mounted one camera on top of a safari vehicle, an attached pole allowing him to quickly move and focus the camera on animals they saw while driving.

In early June the rains began to let up, and wildlife returned to the lake. Every night, elephants came down to its shores. Martin and Osa watched when the moon was bright enough to illuminate the landscape. They saw not only elephants, but rhinoceroses and hyenas arrive for midnight sips of its cool waters. Over time, they became familiar with the wildlife's movements: Buffaloes came at dawn, while the same ten rhinos came every night, including a mother and baby. They recognized five elephants, including a bull with broken tusks that seemed, at times, not to like the looks of their tents.

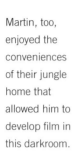
Martin, too, enjoyed the conveniences of their jungle home that allowed him to develop film in this darkroom.

By December, Martin admitted that while this had been the hardest work he had ever done, he never wanted to leave. Osa was "absolutely in love with our home," he confided to a friend. As for himself, he would be happy to spend the remainder of his days in that very spot. Though the nights could be cold, the daytime temperature never rose above 70 degrees Fahrenheit. "The forests are beautiful now," Martin wrote, "the rains are on and everything very green." Though only buffaloes remained around the lake during the rains, Martin was convinced the previous months had gotten him "the greatest elephant film ever made by anyone." "[T]he nice thing is," he continued, "that we are getting the films without

Boculy shows Osa an elephant track as they try to catch up with the migrating herds.

any danger, only twice have we had them get bad." Indeed, Martin and Osa found less reason for using guns on this safari. Martin justified their relative lack of dangerous animal encounters as the natural state of wildlife: If left unmolested, they had no natural reason or instinct to attack humans.

With Boculy tracking for them, Martin and Osa found elephants at every turn. Boculy tediously examined every piece of mud and track, and he could tell by the bend in the grass how recently an elephant had been through. It took three hours for the grass to erect itself fully, he told the Johnsons, and he read the angles of the grass in fifteen-minute intervals. Bent branches meant elephants had been there only a few minutes before. Such knowledge impressed and awed the Johnsons, and over time they began to share Boculy's admiration for the elephants. "Dignified, intelligent, with an apparent awareness of his place in life, this fine animal attends strictly to his own business," observed Osa, "and lets other creatures severely alone."

This "half-brother to the elephants" took them on many walks through the forests around Lake Paradise. One was to the Sunga water hole, three hours away on the border of the surrounding forest and plains. There they camped overnight. Boculy woke Martin and Osa before sunrise to alert them to ten elephants walking past, only four hundred yards away. They rolled out of their cots and walked out into the cool morning air. It was still dark, too dark to photograph, so they simply watched. When the sun began to rise, Martin couldn't resist. He took his camera and filmed them walking along a hillside, their bodies outlined against the horizon. As the sun came up, the rays shone right into his camera, preventing further filming due to overexposure. But Martin, Osa, and Boculy followed this group all day, getting more pictures before scaring them away with their noisy attempts to drive a cobra from the trail.

They visited many idyllic water holes around Lake Paradise, including one they thought among the world's most beautiful. It was enclosed on three sides by tall rocks, the fourth opening out into the valley. It was green on all sides, lush with ferns and vines, and even green in the water, where swamp grass grew. Streams ran out of it and cascaded through the donga. The Johnsons named it Wistonia, using the Swahili word for forest. Boculy wouldn't let the Johnsons enter the donga, however, where they were likely to scare animals with their scent. Instead, they built a blind overlooking the water hole. Kudus came nearby, but not close enough to photograph, and then a rhino and its baby wandered into view. The infant was very young and "still unsteady on its feet," noticed Martin, "but it was as frisky as a kitten. It ran under its mother's belly as she drank; it butted into her; it ran in little jerky steps for a few feet and then back again." The mother drank from the water, but the baby was timid. Osa took still photographs while Martin ground out the scene on film. When darkness fell, they had no regrets. To capture such footage of rhinos at rest was invaluable, making the Johnsons "the happiest people in Africa." They were the "best rhino pictures I have ever made," enthused Martin. At Lake Paradise, they found they did not have to instigate wildlife to obtain good pictures; they could simply present natural glimpses of the animals' private lives.

That same night, Martin and Osa slept in a blind near the water hole, awakening to watch two rhinoceroses drink, then quietly walk off. Soon after they left, the night was filled with the riot of running hooves. They looked out to the water and saw two hundred buffaloes in the water hole, lining the stream all the way into the donga. When they left, Martin went back to sleep, but Osa could not doze off. She wasn't afraid, Martin explained. "She is always too excited and curious." At four in the morning, elephants came to drink, but they didn't stay long. Perhaps detecting a human scent, they ran away, trumpeting. In the morning Martin took pictures of thousands of birds but didn't want to waste his film, so he stopped after a while, though the birds remained. Martin and Osa stayed in the blind all day. Toward evening, a group of half a dozen young male elephants came into sight, and they could hear others breaking their way through the forest. Holding their breaths, Martin and Osa hoped they wouldn't run away again. One group stayed for a while, but they seemed to feel unsafe and went back into the woods. Later that night, some three hundred baboons came to the water hole, and though they seemed to sense something odd, they stayed to drink anyway. In the darkness, all the Johnsons could do was watch. With such good footage from earlier, and no restraints on their time, they were becoming more appreciative of these quiet moments of peaceful observation.

The animals seemed to be catching their scent, so Martin and Osa moved the blind. Their men built a new one of stone, which Martin thought blended in with the landscape better than the mess of leaves and branches of their previous one. He also had the men build a sleeping area constructed of branches a half mile from the blind, so they could sleep away from the photography area and minimize their scent. Leaving the men to their work, Martin and Osa returned to Lake Paradise, where they were reminded they had wildlife right in their own backyard. A group of elephants—males, females, and young—were feeding directly behind Martin's laboratory. They fed and played for two full hours while Martin filmed them. "I'll bet there is no one else on earth who has elephants for scenery right in his back yard," Martin mused.

In addition to the wild animals that roamed through their backyard, Osa had her share of adopted wildlife. Along with Kalowatt, her longtime ape companion, she had brought with her from Nairobi a pair of Persian kittens and a tame cheetah named Marjo, a gift from Percival. Marjo had promptly run off into the forest at Lake Paradise and come home pregnant, giving birth to a litter of four that Osa adoringly named the "polky dots." The kittens and baby cheetahs soon took to each other and played together in Osa's garden. "They were great company for me," mused Osa, who also found companionship in Lazy Bones, a mule she took with her on walks through the forest. It detected nearby animals and pointed like a hunting dog. On one forest walk, Osa found a baby genet cat on a tree limb, and she took it home and named it Spots. Her menagerie was allowed to roam freely about the house and joined the Johnsons at the dinner table, begging for scraps.

Martin credited the friendliness of the wildlife around Lake Paradise to his strict orders that no one shoot a gun in the immediate area. Osa shot game birds for their dinners, but miles away from the lake. Martin was often amused by Osa's tomboy-ish methods of homemaking. When he spied a female elephant near their home, he ran back to grab his camera. Passing the porch, where Osa was sitting, mending a dress, he called to her to grab her gun and come along. "I got a great film and turned to Osa," he said, "she had her half-completed dress thrown over her shoulder, a thimble on one finger, the needle with the thread dangling hanging from her mouth, and her .405 Winchester all ready for action. It struck me as the most ridiculous thing I had ever seen, to see a dress-maker ready to shoot elephants."

Even with the abundant wildlife at their home, Martin and Osa set out on another safari, to a Boran village twelve miles away. They camped just outside the village, waiting for Boculy to lead them to wildlife, but the rains had begun, and the animals were busily shifting around. Martin asked Boculy why the animals were suddenly so elusive, but Boculy did not know. He seemed to know everything about animals, Martin thought, but not the reasons behind their behavior. According to Martin, Boculy would get "very peeved" when asked why an animal did a particular thing. He only knew what they did, not why, and that was good enough for him.

Boculy disappeared for a few days, and when he returned, he said they must wait two more days. Then it rained. Boculy had them pack up and move to another camp, and they walked all morning before arriving at a pool of rainwater. Boculy left them there without explaining why. If Martin and Osa had not learned to trust Boculy so completely, they would have just gone home. After two hours, a pair of Boran men came to fetch them, and they walked for another hour before coming across Boculy, sitting in the shade and casually watching four elephants under a nearby tree. Martin quickly set up his cameras and began to follow them. The group ended up walking back in the moonless dark, Boculy calling out warnings about stones and holes in the way. There was no trail at all. "It was the darkest night I ever knew," said Martin, "but Boculy never once hesitated."

The next day there were more elephants, which Martin thought were the most cooperative yet. They "posed for me in every way I could wish, then in single file they started away parallel with me." He filmed them until they were out of sight, and then he ran forward and did the same again. Osa took stills with one of the Graflex cameras. As the sun began to set, the elephants turned and abruptly began running across the open plains. Martin filmed, thinking how much they looked like Carl Akeley's bronze sculpture at the museum, their hides amber in the setting sun.

By this time, Martin was anxious to return to Lake Paradise to develop his films. Boculy, however, had found another large herd of elephants, and they stayed another three weeks, during which Martin made some of his best elephant films.

Other Westerners on safari were curious about the adventuresome couple living out in the African wilderness, and the Johnsons received several invitations to meet safaris passing nearby. One day a runner came with a request that the Johnsons meet the safari of the Duke and Duchess of York. Osa asked her men to pick some fresh produce from her garden and hurriedly went to manicure her nails, fix her hair, and put on clean clothes and boots. Martin was still busy loading cameras into his car, so Osa, bursting with the chance to meet royalty, drove ahead alone.

It was five hours to the Guaso Nyiro River. When she began to drive across the river, as she had done several times before, she realized the water was higher than usual, and it gushed into the car up to her shoulders. Fortunately, another safari was stalled on the other side of the river. They sent a rope to her, and three men pulled her and her car to land. As Osa frantically looked around for her gift basket of fresh vegetables, a man approached her and asked if she was Mrs. Martin Johnson. She said yes, but she hadn't time to talk. She had to get to Isiolo. A lady with soft blue eyes, the loveliest Osa had ever seen, approached and smiled. "You've had a rather wet crossing, haven't you?" she asked. It was then Osa realized that this was the duke and duchess themselves. She felt very silly for having blundered so badly in front of them, but they took it in stride, biting into her gift of tomatoes from the safely recovered basket.

When Martin arrived, they picnicked at the Isiolo River. The duchess bested Osa in fishing, and the duke caught a crab that he proudly paraded around as a mascot. This made Osa recall her brother's "menagerie" of crawdads, frogs, and turtles, but she dared not tell the duke he reminded her of a little boy. They asked many questions about the Johnsons' work and photography in general and seemed to understand the importance of their project.

———◆———

Martin was kept busy attending not only to filming and developing, but ensuring the proper distribution and promotion of the films. At the American Museum of Natural History, Pomeroy and museum president Henry Fairfield Osborn presented some of the Johnsons' new films to sold-out rooms. So many were interested that they had to schedule two showings—and they still turned about a thousand people away. "I think this makes a record," the museum wrote Martin, "for any showing of pictures or for any lectures at the Museum—even Teddy Roosevelt did not draw a bigger crowd." The films were praised as the best elephant footage ever taken. The only advice the museum people gave the Johnsons was to put more of themselves in the pictures. Audiences wanted to know what it was like to film wildlife in Africa, where Martin and Osa were standing when they took the pictures, and how close the animals really were.

Meanwhile, Osa and Martin were encountering a quickly changing African landscape. While they were traveling for wildlife photos, Martin wrote to Akeley, "It is not the easy job getting pictures that it was four years ago, good roads have brought the Isiolo . . . Archers Post game country within two days of Nairobi and half the safaris come out here." Between Nairobi and Meru, Martin and Osa saw no game at all. It was no wonder. A single safari through the region, they heard, had shot fourteen rhinoceroses, and inexperienced hunters were shooting females and their young. Taxis in Nairobi now offered three-hour tours of game country. The ease of transportation created by the colonial roads and rails, and the growing popularity of automobiles in Kenya, was making once-rugged adventures all but luxurious. A generation that had grown up with tales of Africa like Rider Haggard's *King Solomon's Mines* (1885) and Edgar Rice Burroughs's *Tarzan* (1914), and nonfictional stories of adventure like Roosevelt's *African Game Trails* (1910), was now seeking it out for themselves.

In addition to the growing safari business, native people were being forced off land to make way for settlers, and they began building new villages *(manyettas)* at water holes the animals used to frequent. Hunting for buffalo and giraffe hides and rhino horn was increasing as well. The value of such goods had risen, encouraging more and more desperate natives to turn to the trade to survive. Though the killing of such animals was meant to be monitored by permits, it was difficult to control activities in such unsettled places.

Government stations and new roads were also scaring off game in the Northern Frontier. The British colonial army (King's African Rifles, or KAR) were killing all the elephants, rhinoceroses, and lions they could get a hold of for target practice. The game department, which was supposed to regulate all this, was more interested in collecting fines than in enforcing laws or putting ones into place to stop traders and native hunters. Boer farmers set traps to protect their land, and just one had taken twelve lions, two giraffes, and a rhino. Uganda, said Martin, was considering an elephant hunt to cull their overabundance of the animals. The papers reported they planned to kill ten thousand.

"It is a damn crime, but it can't be stopped," Martin remarked, "and I know that this fine Chobe country will be finished in a few years." Martin told Akeley to keep all of this information confidential, fearful his opinions might interfere with his access in Africa. In another four or five years, he believed, "This Chobe country . . . won't be worth a damn. . . . I can see the game disappearing day by day."

In the spring of 1925, Martin and Osa drove in to Nairobi to meet Akeley, who had assembled a crew of hunters and artists to collect animals and images for the museum's planned hall of African wildlife. While lodged at the Norfolk Hotel, Osa let Kalowatt out the window onto the roof to play while she unpacked. The next thing she knew, the ape was gone. Osa called for her, but to no avail, so she went down to the street, pushing Martin out of her way. When she didn't find her, Osa went back upstairs to see if she'd returned to the hotel room. Looking out the window, Osa saw Kalowatt leaping toward the power lines. When the ape took hold, she was electrocuted. Their intrepid little companion was suddenly no more.

Osa fought back tears as they buried their beloved pet on a hillside outside Nairobi, then quickly went back to the business of preparing for the museum's collecting safari, formally known as the Akeley-Eastman-Pomeroy Expedition. It was organized in a week, but the rains were sure to have flooded the river and ruined the roads to Lake Paradise. It rained well into June, so the impatient party took off on a short trip to the Kedong Valley, thirty-five miles south. The safari consisted of the Johnsons, Mary and Carl Akeley, Daniel Pomeroy, their friend and sponsor George Eastman, and his personal doctor, Audley Stewart. They were also joined by two professional hunters, Pat Ayers and Phillip Percival; the latter, Blayney's brother, was hired by Eastman. After camping in the valley for a few weeks, they headed north to a water hole in the Kaisoot Desert near the Guaso Nyiro River, where Akeley commissioned staff artist William Leigh to make paintings of the landscape to serve as references for the backgrounds of his planned animal dioramas. Leigh was joined by fellow artist Arthur Jansson, who was responsible for capturing the scenes and colors of Africa—something Martin could not do with his camera.

Pomeroy was charged with collecting kudus for the museum hall, Eastman buffaloes, and Osa impalas, while Akeley worked on a mixed-species water hole group. After the animal skins were properly prepared in camp, Akeley and his team of taxidermists at the museum would stuff the animals for the dioramas.

When the river receded, the safari began to move toward Lake Paradise, where Martin and Osa had prepared a special guest-house for Eastman. It looked right out onto the elephant trail, a source of excitement and good photographs. Eastman was experimenting with a new camera he developed, a 16mm cine-camera, but while he may have been a master of the technology, he had much to learn about photography in Africa. Only four days into their safari, he was so involved in photographing a rhinoceros that he walked right up to it without realizing how close he had come. The animal began to snort and looked like it was going to charge. "Never have I seen a greater exhibition of coolness," remarked Osa as she watched him calmly look at the animal and, when it began to charge, step to the side, "like a toreador."

Eastman was a whiz at camp cooking—so much so that even 'Mpishi was awed by his muffins, breads, biscuits, tarts, and pies—and Osa and Eastman became fast friends in the kitchen. He watched her cook and gave her tips on techniques and recipes. "He treated me exactly as though I were a young and slightly unpredictable daughter," Osa thought. "[H]e never could seem to get over what he called my 'pink-silk-dress-little-girlishness,' as contrasted with my ruggedness on safari. . . . [Martin said] he had married me young and trained me that way. And so he had!" Osa thrilled at the company in her Lake Paradise home and busily organized menus and made sure there was plenty of fresh milk and butter from their eleven humpbacked milk cows.

But the expedition needed to move on if they were to collect all the animals Akeley needed for the museum. Martin, Osa, Eastman, and Pomeroy began their way back to Nairobi, stopping leisurely along the way to get pictures and trophy animals. They all met up with Akeley, who was in need of a scenic water hole to inspire the background for the specimens of one diorama. Martin took him to a water hole he thought would be perfect, but after examining all the angles, Akeley thought the background too boring. Martin, who knew this landscape well, had another idea, so they moved

Baking bread in a camp stove, Osa and George Eastman show their shared enjoyment of culinary experimentation.

camp across the Guaso Nyiro River to another water hole, which had views of the mountains. Akeley was delighted. They remained there while the artists sketched and painted the scenery.

The group then went back to Nairobi and prepared for a safari to the Serengeti Plains as they still needed specimens for the museum. Once in camp, however, Akeley felt ill, and he asked Martin to take his place hunting for specimens. Though Martin would rather have taken photographs, he agreed to put down his camera for the good of the museum. Osa hoped being away from his cameras would help him rest a little. She only allowed him to bring one small motion-picture camera, his Eyemo, but once on the plains, he could not ignore his photographer's eye. Every scene was more beautiful, and the light ten times better, than ever before. When he tried to get film of giraffes against a rock outcropping, however, the Eyemo jammed; by the time he reloaded the film, the giraffes were gone. "I was the sickest photographer that ever lived," said Martin, clearly not able to spend a day away from his passion. Pomeroy tried to calm his frustration by getting him interested in the hunt. Though he felled the perfect wildebeest, a Grant's gazelle, and three warthogs for the museum, Martin was still grumpy but, according to Osa, "all puffed up" from his unusual good luck with a gun. Thereafter, Martin refused to shoot in order to maintain this reputation as a master gunman, which both he and Osa knew was not his norm.

Back in camp, Akeley was still sick, so he and his wife, Mary, left for Nairobi, where he could be treated. Martin and Osa stayed with Pomeroy while he collected specimens, but they soon broke camp, anxious to check on Akeley. Though still in the hospital, he was feeling better. The museum work was not yet completed, but Martin and Osa headed back to Lake Paradise for a while. When Akeley was released from the hospital, he and Mary went to Mount Mikeno for gorillas. The group would soon join up again, however, to film the lions of the Serengeti. Reuniting in Nairobi, the Johnsons, the Akeleys, Pomeroy, Eastman, and the rest of the expedition set out into Tanganyika Territory. "A desolate waste in the foothills at the edge of the great plains," said Osa, "it is a rough, practically waterless section and quite different from the northern country."

The Serengeti was known then, as it is now, for its massive herds of game animals. Scouting around camp, Martin and Phillip Percival found herds moving through the area in droves. The migration "[s]tretched far and wide as the eye could see," said Martin. "We all took pictures like mad . . . ," he enthused, awed at the sight of so many animals all in one place. Akeley was focused on lions, and the next day they began searching on the scorching, rocky plains. The heat was so intense, Osa said, that it "fairly frizzed us."

They found a pride of eleven lions that seemed unaffected by their presence. Akeley thought they must be completely undisturbed by the outside world, but Martin doubted that was possible so close to Nairobi. "We hadn't the remotest idea what to expect," said Osa. "All we could do was hope they weren't hungry." Martin and Eastman quickly went to work with their cameras. The lions ignored the human intrusion but seemed to be twitching their ears at the noises from the cameras. They looked over once when Osa spoke, but otherwise they were uninterested and responded with contagious yawns. Osa broke out in a rash of goose bumps waiting to see what they would do, but the lions simply rolled over and slept.

Later on, a twelfth lion, larger than the others, joined the pride. He woke them up playfully, but the drowsy lions moaned and growled in irritation. Soon the twelfth lion also laid down and slept, comically rolling his feet straight up into the air. The humans quietly left them to their nap and picnicked in the shade of a mimosa. Akeley was thrilled that his theory that lions do not attack humans for no cause seemed true.

The peaceful existence of lions and humans was interrupted, ironically, by the spear-hunting film commissioned by the museum. Pomeroy and Akeley wanted a record of the native Lumbwa lion hunt, and the Johnsons consented to film it. They gathered forty Lumbwa and brought them to the Serengeti Plains to film the scenes. Because a truly authentic native hunt might not have catered to the needs of the camera, Eastman, the Akeleys, and the Johnsons drove around in their cars, trying to scare the lions into the light. The lions wanted none of this affair and hid in a dark donga. After a few days, the Lumbwa successfully surrounded a lion out in the open and speared him.

These films secured, the Akeley-Pomeroy-Eastman Expedition disbanded. They were in Nairobi in the fall of 1926 when Pomeroy helped Martin and Osa purchase a house in the suburb of Muthaiga. The gray stone building was surrounded by gardens, which pleased Osa, had modern heating and refrigeration, and eight rooms. Even though they were elated to own their first real home, the Johnsons could not relax completely. Their good friend Akeley was sick again, and Eastman was about to leave for

Lumbwa natives encircle their lion kill at the end of their ritual hunt.

America. Osa remembered his words as he boarded the train for his long trek home: "Back to the world of fraud and front."

The Johnsons went back to Lake Paradise, but only to close down their home there. Feeling better, Akeley went back to Mount Mikeno, but he never returned—he died on the mountain among his beloved gorillas. Stricken with grief at the loss of their good friend and supporter who had earned them the museum's support and first pointed them toward Africa, Martin decided they must honor his memory by continuing to study the lions he believed were more gentle than their reputation allowed.

George Eastman transported several reels of Martin's films, giving them to the museum upon his arrival in New York. A team of film editors, script writers, and museum experts crafted Martin's incredible lion footage into a feature film, *Simba* (1928). This collaboration of field footage, story writing, and expert oversight created an authentic view of Africa. It was, as one ad proclaimed, "Not a staged or movie production . . . but Africa as God made it."

Simba found audiences through its story of adventure and endorsement by the American Museum of Natural History.

THRILLS! EXCITEMENT! ADVENTURE! LAUGHS! promised the advertisements for the Johnsons' new film. The promotional material stressed the dangers of making the film, the "breathtaking" scenes, and the impression that it was suitable for young viewers (i.e., no scantily clad natives or inappropriate sexuality). The *New York World* called *Simba,* "Without doubt the greatest big game hunting picture ever made." *Simba* played for over a month in some theaters. The American Museum of Natural History— who had, in part, sponsored the film—offered to give its employees tickets, but even they had trouble getting them. The first week was completely sold out, and theater managers didn't know when more tickets would be available.

Though Martin and Osa were in Africa when the film was released in January 1928, the media hungered for news of them and their ongoing adventures. They were featured in dozens of newspaper articles and several newsreels. Martin's articles and photographs glossed the pages of popular magazines such as *Scientific American, New York Times Magazine,* and the *Saturday Evening Post.* Osa's stories landed in *Good Housekeeping* and *Collier's.*

American audiences became increasingly intrigued by African tales and films during the course of the 1920s. Beginning in 1921, several *Tarzan* films treated audiences to the fiction and romance of the African jungle and enjoyed box office success. Rider Haggard's novel *King Solomon's Mines* (1885), generally considered the first African novel, was made into a silent film in 1920. Other seemingly less fictional films, *With Stanley in Africa* (1922) and *Wild Men of Africa* (1921), created a landscape of African adventure that lured audiences into theaters.

———

Even before *Simba*'s 1928 release, the Johnsons had been looking for a different kind of African adventure. A few months after the end of the Akeley-Eastman-Pomeroy Expedition, Martin and Osa decided to climb Mount Kenya. Martin was excited at the thought of capturing photographs of its white, icy glaciers. They would be, he thought, an "interesting contrast to the tropical life below." The Johnsons organized thirty porters, headmen, gun bearers, and an American driver and mechanic, John Wilsheusen, who had accompanied Pomeroy and Eastman, and drove off toward the mountain.

On January 16, 1927, Martin and Osa arrived at Chogoria Mission, on the slopes of the mountain. There, a mission physician, Dr. Irwine, and his wife, helped them find fifty more Meru porters for their ascent. They stayed only one night, then began the trek upward. The porters, with their heavy loads, needed to rest every half hour, and the going was slow. It was difficult climbing, but the "forests of fairy-like beauty" made up for it, at least to Osa. They camped in a wildflower-filled clearing on the edge of a bamboo forest. It was colder than they had anticipated, so Wilsheusen went back for more blankets for the porters, who were ill-prepared for such weather. "[W]e had forgotten," admitted Osa, "just how cold ice and snow and high altitude could be."

In the morning they tackled the bamboo forest, which seemed an endless expanse of sameness. The bamboo grew to fifty feet tall, darkening the path and making the end invisible. Once on the other side, Osa stood enchanted. "[W]e found ourselves in some of the most beautiful country I have ever seen," she described, "great rolling mountain plains with groves of scrub trees, all fantastically hung with Spanish moss and with Mount Kenya towering above it in all its rugged and almost forbidding beauty." Martin agreed it was some of the most attractive country he had ever seen.

On the third day, Martin could not get comfortable; he was hot and cold all at the same time. They reached the timberline at 12,000 feet above sea level, where a hut remained from an eccentric millionaire's plan to build a road up to the top of the mountain. Even though they burrowed under six blankets apiece, they were still too chilled to sleep. In the morning, Osa found Martin burning with fever, but he did not want to turn back. They stayed in camp to rest for a day, then tried to move on, but as they ascended, the altitude made them short of breath and weak. They stayed that night on a ridge where Martin took pictures, but they were both so tired that they went to bed without dinner. Osa woke up sick in the middle of the night, and Martin was still burning up, too. They tried to treat themselves by drinking warm whiskey and placing hot water bottles between their bedsheets, but their ailments only worsened. Martin desperately wanted pictures of the top of the mountain and refused to backtrack. He sent porters down for more kerosene for the lamps and hoped to wait the illness out.

When Wilsheusen heard of the state of things on the mountain, he jumped in the Willys-Knight and drove all the way to where they were encamped. The road did not extend past the rest house at 12,000 feet, but he cut trail with the car up the mountain, carrying it with the porters when necessary. When he saw Osa, he knew immediately from her shortness of breath that she had pneumonia. Wilsheusen put them each on stretchers and loaded them into the car, which slid and tipped as it went down the mountain. To keep it from completely sliding out of control, the porters held it back as they descended the steepest stretches and balanced it on crooked ground. Though ill, Martin and Osa had to rouse themselves several times to get out of the car for the men to carry it. Martin hated doing it—not so much for himself, but for Osa, who he thought was on death's door.

By nightfall they were back at the mission, where Dr. Irwine diagnosed Osa with double pneumonia and Martin with influenza and bronchitis. Osa felt better, but Martin's temperature was rising. Then Osa worsened, becoming so ill that she was delirious. Wilsheusen called for a doctor from Nairobi, then drove the 165 miles to get a nurse. When he returned to the mission, the doctor requested medicine and another nurse, so Wilsheusen got back in the car and immediately drove to Nairobi again. When he returned again, the doctors said they would be much better off if they had an ice machine so they could keep the feverish pair constantly cooled. Without hesitation, Wilsheusen again drove to the city to fetch one. His heroic efforts no doubt saved the Johnsons' lives.

Martin stayed in the mission while Osa was being treated by medical professionals in another hut. Late one night, or very early in the morning—Martin could not remember which—the doctor came into his room and told him he was afraid Osa would not make it to daylight. Martin went to the hut, where the doctors were applying cold wet towels to Osa's forehead. "[I]t was the most heart breaking sight I ever saw . . . ," grieved Martin, "Osa was unconscious . . . her eyes wide open, her lips a ghastly blue and her breathing was so fast that it was horrible . . . then she would start coughing and gasp for breath . . . after each coughing spell she seemed to be dying." The doctor sent a telegraph to Osa's mother, preparing her for the worst.

In the morning Osa seemed better, but Martin was still so worried that he kept checking on her. The doctors ordered him back to bed, for he was not fully recovered himself. From his room he heard her coughing spells, and he could not resist going to her. Amazingly, she recovered. In the end, all Osa could recall during her illness were the haunting sounds of the missionaries' bells and chanting.

They rested for six more weeks at the mission before Martin urged Dr. Irwine to let them leave the cool, damp air of the mountain, thinking Osa would do better elsewhere. But a flu epidemic had hit Nairobi, and he forbade them from endangering themselves to further illness. Instead the doctor agreed to let them go on a restful safari to the plains, where the sun, dry air, and movement might revive Osa's lungs and spirits. They camped at Embayo, near Meru, where they could gaze upon the wildlife they loved. Martin got back to filming while Osa, assisted by a nurse, Sister Withall, worked on getting the strength to simply walk again. In a few weeks she was miraculously back by Martin's side, with her gun at the ready.

It had been an eventful four years in Africa, and Martin and Osa had gathered an abundant amount of film footage. The time had come to head to New York, where they would turn that footage into commercial and scientific films. On the way they stopped in Paris, where Osa purchased the latest fashions in gowns and hats, which would soon earn her accolades among the American fashion world.

They arrived in New York on May 16, 1927, into the welcoming arms of their families, who had come from Kansas, as well as their city friends. In their absence, the Johnsons had grown even more popular with American audiences. Offers for their appearances poured in, promising upward of $100,000. They even embraced the idea of doing live radio broadcasts, and Osa did at least one that her friends in Kansas heard live. "[S]he was scared stiff," Martin revealed. Throughout the summer, Martin and Osa painstakingly worked on *Simba* and could not get away from New York, making Martin swear that he would never make a feature film again. Instead, they would go back to lecturing and become wealthy celebrities with more time to themselves.

This, however, did not come from Martin's heart. After their long sojourn in Africa, Martin and Osa found themselves much changed, and the values of American life were no longer their own. They honestly cared little for fame and money, despite Osa's fashionable attire. "[W]hen you live in Africa, down close to the earth and the animals, you acquire a different set of values from when you live in the city," they agreed. Even Osa, said Martin, was less materialistic than she used to be. "[J]ust to get back into my Safari clothes again," she said, "Oh! How happy I will be."

When George Eastman invited them to go back to Africa with him, they did not hesitate. "Our business associates thought we were crazy to turn down such wonderful opportunities to fatten our bank account," confessed Martin, "and said so without mincing words." But Martin replied, "[L]ife is much too short for all the work we've set out to do . . . I guess money isn't very important to Osa and me. . . . This resulted in a chorus of protests: Money was important to everybody. What could we hope to accomplish without money?"

In December they boarded a boat for Paris with Eastman. Osa's mother was there to see them off and had dinner with some of their sophisticated New York friends. Thinking ahead to Christmas, Osa again felt homesick during the trip across the Atlantic, but she made the best of it, buying presents for everyone in various European cities and dancing all night in Nice, France, at a party hosted by Eastman's friends. They whirled their way through Genoa, Berlin, London, Paris, Monte Carlo, and Cairo. Martin and Osa saw Eastman's humanitarian side when together they visited several dental clinics for underprivileged children, which he financed in England and Italy.

Despite all the globe-trotting, Osa's letters to her mother sounded listless. She confessed to crying every night. "I am very lonely and down hearted," she wrote her mother. "I grieved so bad when we left home that just above my heart above my left breast a red round mark just like a wound appeared [*sic*] wasn't that queer?" In Paris, where she had thrilled at the latest fashions just months earlier, she now bought nothing at all. Martin seemed to sense her mood and tried to cheer her up with extravagant lingerie. "Martin is so sweet to me," she told her mother, but the gift didn't seem to help.

At Port Said, Eastman charted a steamer to take them down the Nile. The boat, the *Dal,* had twenty-seven staterooms for their party of only four, and the crew and stewards had separate rooms as well. Eastman installed an electric refrigerator and packed cases of mineral water, along with live chickens, goats, and sheep. They steamed past the ancient ruins of Luxor and the Valley of the Kings, then up the White Nile to Khartoum, where they met up with fellow filmmaker Merian Cooper, who was filming a war drama, *The Four Feathers.* They stayed a few days, and then Cooper filmed them departing up the Nile.

They now headed to the Upper Nile, where Martin found gazelle, elephants, crocodiles, and even hippopotamuses to photograph. On one stretch of the river thousands of perch floated belly-up; while they never learned the true mystery of the fishes' deaths, they were told it was caused by an earthquake.

Phillip Percival met Eastman, Osa, and Martin at Rejaf, Sudan, from where they headed down to the Belgian Congo. There Eastman planned to shoot an elephant and a white rhinoceros—two prizes for the museum he had failed to get on his first expedition. Eastman, now seventy-five years old, again had a personal doctor, Albert Kaiser, at his side. Under Kaiser's advice, they hired several additional porters to carry bottled water and constructed an umbrella-covered sedan chair in which Eastman could be carried. While Eastman tracked down his two specimens, Martin and Osa filmed white rhinoceroses—one of the rarest animals in Africa at the time. They drove back to Rejaf, where Eastman boarded the *Dal,* his eyes filled with tears. He said it was "the happiest period of my life," and he told them to take care of each other, though he was sure they would.

Osa and Martin then returned to the Belgian Congo, where they visited an elephant-training camp, and then went to the Ituri Forest to search for native pygmies. The Mbuti (Osa called them Wambutti) people allowed the Johnsons to film them. Martin was particularly happy with the unusual but charming pictures of women feeding the chief rolled balls of rice and sugar one by one. Finding these diminutive people friendly and interesting, Martin and Osa decided they would come back someday to record more of their culture.

Next they sailed up the Victoria Nile to Murchison Falls, getting their best hippopotamus pictures yet. The falls were "magnificent," said Osa, who seemed to be less homesick as they neared Nairobi. They stayed in the home they had purchased near the city, in Muthaiga, and prepared for a lion safari.

As Martin had promised himself when Akeley passed away, he would continue to investigate Akeley's lions in the Tanganyika Territory. On their safari, they set up camp on the plains with just five tents, food, water, and medicine. The bulk of their load was their photography equipment—ten motion cameras, eleven still cameras, and one hundred thousand feet of film.

"We worked with lions," explained Osa, "we ate and slept with their roars all around us." Their reputation for ferocity was not true, she asserted. Lions were part of "man's dread of Africa," but "curiously enough, [man] is the only enemy the lion really fears." Hunting encroached on lions' sense of safety, but they did not randomly retaliate. Though some hunting restrictions were in place in the region, both Martin and Osa hoped the Serengeti Plain would someday be set aside as a game preserve.

Their feelings for lions mingled love and fear. "For the most part, the lion is a thoroughly agreeable personage," explained Osa. "He lives a most leisurely existence, loafs and sleeps a great deal, has just as playful moods as a house cat, and is just as decided a personality. He minds his own business, is very fond of his family, and takes his duties as a family protector very seriously." She watched the young males roaming about "having a hilarious time," she thought, before they would settle down to "domestic bliss" (much as Martin had done).

Martin and Osa filmed groups of lions as they lounged, wrestled, romped, and slept. They found the wild cats curious but not harmful. One young male, who decided to run apace with their car, looked disappointed when they came to a stop in order to scare him away. He had liked the game, Osa thought, shrugged (as much as a lion could shrug), and came up with a new one. He approached the car, sniffed the tire, then tried to sink his teeth into it. He did not, however, like the taste of rubber. Then the lion pawed it, trying to make some sort of game out of the odd object. Seeing more lions grow curious about the game, Martin and Osa thought they had best get rid of their playmate. Osa raced the engine, thinking the noise would startle him, but he just stood there and cocked his head, trying to figure it out. When he got a taste of the car fumes, however, he looked rather displeased. Deciding his investigations were complete, he ran off.

The film Martin envisioned would include complete footage of both the diurnal and nocturnal habits of lions. Though Martin had taken night photos of wildlife with flashlights and cameras rigged to go off with snares (not to trap the animal, but to trigger the shot), he wanted to work the cameras himself. He planned to take the car out at night, with cameras, lights, and an electric torch.

First, however, they had to have bait. Both Martin and Osa had come to find shooting zebras for bait unpleasant and tedious, so Osa tried to offload the task on Martin by telling him he should do it since he hadn't done enough shooting. "[A]s long as I'm the only cameraman around here and you're the one hold-ing the gun," Martin teased back, "I think you should keep in practice." They were now old hands at being on safari. The ani-mals still intrigued them, but camp life and hunting were mere routines of existence.

Their car now loaded with cameras and lighting equipment, and the bait properly placed, Martin and Osa drove out onto the plains. While Martin slept, Osa listened carefully to the sounds in the night. When she heard something, she pinched Martin to wake him. He grabbed the electric torch, and they saw a large male lion tearing the zebra apart. Martin clicked the camera, but the light attached to the car roof did not go off as it should. When the lion looked up, Osa pointed her gun at his head, but he roared a warning and went back to eating. Martin climbed to the top of the car as quietly as he could to fix the flash. Soon females and smaller lions approached, and the male let them eat from the kill as well. To ensure Martin's safety, Osa honked the horn and shone the lights into their faces. Better to scare off the lions than have them leap toward them, startled at the noise. The females and young lions backed away, but the large male suddenly noticed the camera and started gnawing on its base. Martin yelled instinc-tively and started to throw rocks at the lion while Osa shot her gun into the air. But this was to no avail; the lions seemed scared of nothing, and strangely, they seemed more interested in cameras and cars than humans.

When Martin and Osa took pictures in the daytime, a group of playful young males completely ignored them, but when they took their picnic lunches to the roof of the car, the lions grew curi-ous. The pride came over and sat down, said Osa, "like a bunch of hungry beggars," and she threw them partridge legs, which they quickly devoured. Then they played with the tires and wrestled with each other right next to the car.

As Martin and Osa watched the group play, they began to see personalities emerge, the lions reminding them of people they knew.

They named the animals accordingly: The most well-groomed lion they called Roy Chapman Andrews, after the explorer; the loudest was Lowell Thomas, after the broadcaster; the most interested in rubber was George Dryden, investor and rubber merchant; and the wisest was Merian Cooper, fellow filmmaker. Among the lions, they saw familiar character types—the clown, the nobleman, the flirt, the egotist—and tried to catch those on film.

It became clear on that safari that Martin and Osa were finally done with unnecessary hunting. Osa continued to hunt for food, but she was no longer interested in the thrill of sport. In fact, she killed only one lion in their entire year on the plains, and that was out of self-defense. Martin had startled a sleeping lion one day while setting up his camera. The lion jumped up and faced them, showing warning signs—drawn-back ears, lashing tail, and a threatening snarl—but Martin, cigar in mouth, continued to carelessly fidget with the camera. Osa took up her gun, but Martin said the lion was bluffing even when it growled as it approached them. As Martin began to crank the camera, the lion crouched, then charged. Osa shot, but feeling a bit dazed, was startled to see the animal fall, midleap, just thirteen feet in front of them.

Their year in lion country was interrupted by at least one trip to Nairobi—to pick up three Boy Scouts who had won a contest to join the famous adventurers on safari. The contest was a publicity push by Martin's publisher, George Palmer Putnam, to promote sales of Martin's book *Lion*. Putnam was known for recruiting explorers to publish their "true-life adventures" and had already enlisted adventurers Knud Rasmussen and William Beebe, as well as aviators Charles Lindbergh and Amelia Earhart. Though Martin had already published *Safari*, about their time at Lake Paradise, Putnam saw the possibilities of a book centered around filming the alluring cats of Africa. *Lion* recounts Martin and Osa's work on the African plains with the eponymous animals the subtitle dubs "the King of Beasts." The fifteen-year-old Boy

Scouts, Dick Douglas, Dave Martin, and Douglas Oliver, spent five weeks on safari and were treated to Martin and Osa's intimate knowledge of lions, rhinoceroses, and elephants.

The boys were good companions for the Johnsons and their crew, and they impressed the natives with their skills, often besting them at their own trades. The Boy Scouts were better with bows and arrows and taught the natives the sport of wrestling. Osa was pleased with the young men and wrote of their visit as "diverting and extremely pleasant." Everyone was sorry to see them go.

Martin and Osa returned to New York once again to promote their work. Where before they used to beg for support, now they were such famous and respected personages that they were handed gifts. Automobile manufacturer Walter Chrysler offered Osa one of his cars, but she unfortunately had to refuse; they had a contract with Willys-Knight, the manufacturer of the vehicles they used on safari.

Martin finished his book *Lion* with the help of Fitzhugh Green, who also wrote a biography of Martin for young readers entitled *Martin Johnson: Lion Hunter.* Both books were published in 1929 by Putnam. Osa began packaging her *Good Housekeeping* articles for another Putnam publication, *Jungle Babies,* released the next year. "We work harder and longer hours than anyone in the country," Martin said, "but we have the satisfaction of knowing that it is getting us somewhere, and in knowing that we will be able to finance our next and biggest expedition we have made."

They toured with a lecture film called *Adventuring Johnsons* but were in such high demand they grew exhausted with the work. "Life is just one dam [*sic*] theatre after another," said Martin, "and we are sick of being actors . . . but we have Africa to look forward to." The money they earned and raised would go to their next expedition—deep into the Congo forest. They secured a contract with the movie studio Fox for release of their next commercial film, in which they planned to include the latest Hollywood craze—sound.

Thus they once again sailed from New York, this time with George Dryden and his son, George Eastman Dryden (the son of George Eastman's niece), who were going hunting in Africa. For their own crew the Johnsons brought sound engineers recommended by Fox studios and DeWitt Sage, the son of an investor who had previously traveled in Africa with the museum's curator of birds, James P. Chapin. They traveled around Europe together, seeing London, Paris, and Berlin. Despite being the belle of the ball in a new pale-blue and gold lace evening gown, Osa wrote to her mother, "It is very long and [has] wonderful lines, but in spite of being made so much over I wasn't happy." Apparently, during their time at Lake Paradise, Osa had begun to drink regularly to combat the loneliness caused by being away from her mother and other female companionship. However, Osa told her mother that now she was only drinking beer. "I am keeping my promise pretty good," she confided, "[t]hanks to you."

Osa tried to write a story about Kalowatt but couldn't concentrate or find inspiration. She felt disgusted by the living conditions of the people in Egypt, where she recoiled at the dirt, disease, and poverty. "I don't quite know just what has happened to me," Osa expressed to her mother, wondering where her thrill of seeing new places had gone, "but I feel so new and different, as if nothing mattered now, and as if my soul was as blank as the Sahara desert." She longed to talk to her mother, and the thought of two years without her seemed "to me like going to the end of the earth." Perhaps it was the fact that she lived mostly among men that made Osa subject to homesickness. There were few women for Osa to confide in during her travels; the few that did accompany expeditions only did so temporarily. All of the Johnsons' workers were male. She found occasional companionship with native African women, but it does not appear they were a permanent part of safari life. The lack of female companionship in Osa's life was beginning to take its toll.

For such an avid adventurer, her letters to her mother seem odd and out of place. Never in the field does she seem quite so listless. Perhaps such bouts of depression were brought on by the ocean, its wide, open expanse known for making people more introspective. Osa enjoyed the view of the ocean from the ship, but the breaking waves seemed to share her conflict between her longing for home and her desire for adventure. "The sun is shining so beautifully," she wrote, "and these great waves of deep blue water seem to be so restless and discontented with themselves—they seem to be always seeking some new kind of adventure."

When they arrived in Nairobi, Osa found inspiration at last in fixing up their Muthaiga home. Decorating and gardening consumed her time, and she was touched by Dryden's gift of a fancy radio for their living room. She spent Christmas trout fishing—one of her favorite pastimes—and impressed everyone with her marksmanship at the shooting range. Back in her element, Osa told her mother, "before I leave this country I will take on some animal charging, and I will make the world set [sic] up and take notice." The thrill of being back in Africa lifted Osa's spirits and brightened her mood. "[N]ow the sun is just beginning to shine again for me," Osa wrote. "Oh! Mother dear how long I have waited for that. Every thing seemed so black and forlorn—but now it is much brighter."

———— ◆ ————

Once again settled in Africa, at the start of 1930, the Johnsons prepared to film their first motion pictures with sound. Instead of heading directly into the Congo, they began on more familiar ground—Tanganyika's plains. The Drydens had seen *Simba* in New York and wanted to see the great "lion's den" for themselves. They were good safari companions, patient with the weather and the insects. The elder Dryden was a great hunter and, Osa said, "always cool when we were in a dangerous spot."

Despite all their previous peaceful experiences with wild cats, when the safari came upon their first lion, it charged. Osa, not expecting such aggressive behavior, was playing with a loose button on her shirt, so George Dryden stepped in and shot the animal on the spot. They all teased Osa mercilessly for not living up to her reputation as a crack shot. The safari moved on to the rugged Abyssinian border, where Osa redeemed herself by shooting a charging rhino. "[W]e have never had a finer nor more agreeable companion in all our travels," she admitted of George Dryden.

After the Drydens left, Martin and Osa prepared for their trip into the Belgian Congo. They had seven Willys-Knights, including two equipped as camera cars ready to get sound recordings as they drove, one set up as a mobile darkroom, and one outfitted with beds, a stove, and all their essentials. When they loaded the cars and equipment onto the train to Torero, Uganda, Osa laughed, "We resembled one of those small one-ring circuses that toured our own Middle West." After the jerks and noise of the narrow-gauge railroad, Osa was glad to be back in the car "and to feel that, for a time at least, I could control my own destiny."

They drove for four days to Guiana on Lake Albert, a "wretched, barren, steaming village," and loaded the equipment onto a barge to cross the lake. They had to take a steamer, the *Samuel Baker,* which was not yet there, so they visited Murchison Falls to take pictures—with sound—of the "roaring, raging" falls and "the noisy, often raucous sounds of the animals." When they returned to the lake, the steamer was waiting. With the barge in tow, they crossed thirty miles over what they thought was "one of the roughest bodies of water in the world."

Once on land, they began the drive to Irumu, on the eastern edge of the Ituri Forest. The road was good but steep. After a few days, they met two Mbuti pygmies on the road, the local chief Deelia and his son, Salou. "Deelia was a sixty-pound, bewhiskered, agile old chap whose height was something like three feet ten inches," said Osa. "His perfectly formed body was covered with hair, and his only garments were a crude bead necklace and a loincloth of bark." Salou was "a fat, active fellow" and taller than his father by a full foot. Not understanding why Martin and Osa would want to camp near the village, they conferred with Bwana Sura, a nonpygmy native African who had somehow gained power among the people. Acting as translator, Bwana Sura convinced the men to host the strange guests, and they organized men to clear land in the forest where the Johnsons could set up their tents.

Deelia, Salou, and Bwana Sura brought pygmies to the Johnsons' camp each day. Their forest village was too dark for Martin to film, so they set up an impromptu village in a brighter spot, which eventually grew until there were about thirty pygmies encamped around the Johnson safari. Bwana Sura tried to get Martin to pay him for bringing the people in, but Martin refused and soon kicked the presumptuous man out of camp. Many more pygmies were gathered in the forest, and Martin did his best to bring them to camp, where lighting was better for his pictures, but they were afraid of the cars. At last they consented, swayed by Martin's friendliness, but they were still wary of riding in the cars and sang nervously the whole way to camp.

When they arrived, however, they wouldn't get out of the cars. Martin and Osa persuaded them with their usual gifts of rice, tobacco, calico, and salt. "They were beautifully formed little people," Osa felt, "with clear skins and well-shaped bodies and heads." They dressed in loincloths of calico; some wore beaded necklaces. Martin and Osa coaxed Chief Deelia to begin a dance, and all the men and women soon joined in, either dancing or drumming, the men holding bows and arrows.

Though the people were rather shy and liked to remain in the depths of the forest, Osa was able to coax the women into showing her their methods of cooking. They ate mostly rice and

Martin plays his phonograph for Mbuti pygmies.

bananas and had only clay pots in which to prepare meals. "The domestic life of these people is clean, wholesome, admirable," she said. Martin and Osa learned about their customs, as well. They had no religion, it seemed, and "gave no thought to the hereafter and very little more to the present." There were no burials or skulls, and they could not figure out what the people did with their dead. They were lucky enough to take pictures of a wedding ceremony and learned these people stayed together for life. Their only vice was a banana beer that sent the whole village on "hilarious spree[s]."

"Theirs, it might be said, was a Utopian existence," mused Osa, "for they showed neither hate, greed, vanity, envy, nor any other of the dominatingly unpleasant emotions of our so-called civilized world." Martin, Osa, and their soundmen took a complete record of these people's lives before the pygmies grew tired of the heat of the Johnsons' camp and wanted to return to the "constant twilight of the forest" and their usual diet of wild greens, grubs, insects, and the occasional monkey or elephant.

Having secured their pygmy photos, Martin and Osa began to prepare for their gorilla expedition to Mount Mikeno in the Virunga Mountains. They paused in Rutshuru, where they purchased food for the trip and found porters and guides. Anxious to get to cooler temperatures, they began their safari. They stopped at the Lubenga Mission, where five fathers and four nuns were stationed in a complex comprising schools, dwellings, a church, and flower and vegetable gardens. The missionaries gave them a house to rest in. They were on the edge of Parc National Albert (now Virunga National Park), which had been established in 1925. The fathers praised Akeley and Belgian officials for preserving the land, which was Africa's first national park.

Osa saw her first gorilla early one morning while looking for wild celery. She was in a field that was full of it and took a bite, which she promptly spit out because of its bitter taste. As she did so, a large gorilla grunted behind her, and she turned to see him. She ran fifty yards right into Martin, who had come looking for her. Though she ran, the gorilla hadn't charged; he had simply looked at her.

"Making pictures of gorillas isn't what it's cracked up to be," said Osa. She and Martin could hear the elusive gorillas everywhere, "but by the time we had climbed through the cold mists and rains and thick, sopping jungle growth to where we had heard them, they were gone, usually, beyond our view." The altitude shortened their breath, the cold chilled their bones, and the endless search for gorillas exhausted them. Even when they caught up to gorillas, the light of the forest was usually so dark that they couldn't get pictures.

Walking through the forest, even on flat terrain, was difficult as the ground was a mess of vines and vegetation. Their guide, Bukhari, seemed unaffected by the hardships, however. He found tunnels through the vegetation that had been made by gorillas and led the safari through them, usually finding a group at the end, eating or nesting. Though their muscles were sore from crawling through the tunnels all day, the good pictures more than made up for the discomfort.

Bukhari suggested they go to the Alimbongo Mountains, just west of the Virunga range, for more gorilla pictures. On the way, Martin and Osa visited Carl Akeley's grave, in the saddle of Mount Mikeno, the mountain he had loved. The climb was difficult and steep, and the rain soaked their clothes, but as they neared the grave, the sun shone through the clouds and lit up the surrounding mountains in bright shades of green, yellow, and purple. Martin repaired Akeley's grave, a simple monument, and its fence while Osa planted ferns and vines, and made a wreath of wildflowers that she placed on the grave just before they left.

They hired Akeley's old guide, Magollo, to take them to a view Akeley had told them he adored. Fog hung over the horizon when they arrived, so they built a fire and hoped to be able to wait it out. Clouds teased them with glimpses but filled the view in again. They waited for three hours, and then, suddenly, the clouds cleared. In the distance, they could see smoke from volcanoes, Lake Kivu, and rolling mountains for fifty miles around. "The scene [that] unrolled before our enraptured gaze," wrote Martin, "was a magnificent panorama, noble, majestic, and overpowering in its effect." This view, in all its "wild beauty," was painted by William Leigh, who had accompanied the Akeley-Eastman-Pomeroy Expedition, as the background to Akeley's gorilla group at the American Museum of Natural History's exhibition which was, after his death, named after the explorer, Akeley Hall of African Mammals.

In the village of Kibondo, 8,000 feet above sea level on the slopes of the Alimbongo Mountains, native farmland weaved in among the thick jungle. Gorillas were such a common sight to these people that they didn't understand Martin and Osa's interest in them. Martin asked if gorillas were as ferocious as he had heard. Did they really carry off women and children into the forest? No, said the people, this was all nonsense. They eyed him suspiciously for even asking.

Back in America, people would not have found such a question out of place. Since the nineteenth century, reports credited to Paul du Chaillu, who published fantastic tales of the beasts and claimed to be the first white man to ever see them with his own eyes, bombarded American audiences with images of gorilla ferocity. In 1930 the film *Ingagi* embodied all these negative images in what producer William S. Campbell claimed was a documentary set in the Congo. The film featured a native tribe who worshipped a six-hundred-pound gorilla and included a scene of a ritual virgin sacrifice to the beast. Though clearly a hoax, the film thrilled audiences. Only later was it proven that the scenes were filmed on Hollywood sets and the footage featuring the gorilla was in fact a combination of a man in a monkey suit and an orangutan from a zoo. The film's fakery angered American scientists and conservationists who were trying to garner sympathy for what they believed were quite gentle creatures. When Merian Cooper released *King Kong* three years later, he played upon these myths while characterizing the goals of scientific filmmakers, like the Johnsons, who sought the truth.

Martin asked such questions because he not only wanted to get pictures of the apes, he also wished to bring one back to the United States. A living specimen, he thought, would help to debunk the myths. He had obtained a permit from the Belgian government to capture a gorilla, and Martin asked the village chief, Pawko, to round up a crew of hunters who could assist him in trapping one. Pawko quickly called in seventy-five men and a pack of mangy dogs, claiming the latter were "gorilla hounds," a statement even Bukhari found ridiculous.

Neither dogs nor men seemed to know how to begin a gorilla hunt. Martin led the way, and they soon came to a gorilla trail. The men and dogs began to make noise, and Martin told them to pipe down, but Pawko said the gorilla was used to such noises. Pawko had a plan: He gathered the men in a semicircle and placed the leashed dogs in the center, but when unleashed, they ran back to the village. Pawko then sent half of the hunters to search the forest and the other half to clear undergrowth in a one-hundred-yard area. Martin and Osa were skeptical. After two hours, the searchers ran into the cleared area, hollering, but they looked around to discover that the gorillas they thought they had scared up were not there. Pawko said he had a new plan, but the Johnsons, with a mix of annoyance and amusement, left for camp.

Abandoning their quest to capture a great ape, Martin and Osa went back to filming. One day, however, while they were walking through the forest, they came across a group of young gorillas accompanied by a six-foot silverback (as elder male gorillas are called for the silver hair that develops down their backs). Without thinking, they chased the silverback, but he reared and charged toward them. When they stopped, he retreated, pounded his chest, and "screeched with frenzy." They watched him for a while before he went into the forest, leaving behind two of the smaller gorillas, which panicked and quickly climbed a tree.

With cameras and sound rolling, Martin organized the hunters to cut down the surrounding trees, in order to isolate the apes and give them no source of escape. They cleared the ground and stood in a circle, and then chopped at the tree holding the gorillas. Martin and Sage bundled themselves in coats and gloves, preparing to wrestle the gorillas when they hit the ground. The gorillas screamed all the while.

Osa cranked the camera, feeling sorry for the trapped animals. She thought they might be "sweethearts" as one seemed to be protecting the other. The tree fell, and Bukhari grabbed one ape and wrapped it in a tarp. Three other men ran after the other gorilla and caught it. Even though they only had a permit to capture one gorilla and now had two, they picked up another along the road—a sick infant Osa named Snowball. All three survived the trip to the United States. They gave Congo and Ngagi (as Osa named the first two) to the San Diego Zoo, and Snowball, who had become Osa's beloved pet, to the National Zoo in Washington, D.C.

———

Back in New York, Martin and Osa visited the nearly complete African Hall at the American Museum of Natural History. "[W]e marveled at the wonder of it all," said Martin. They spent hours looking at the dioramas of stuffed animals, natural vegetation, and painted backgrounds. They stood in front of the water hole group they had helped obtain with Pomeroy and Eastman, admiring its view, which Martin had handpicked for Akeley. They were amazed at the realism of the plains group containing Martin's wildebeest and Grant's gazelle. The background was so detailed, they could pick out exact locations where they had camped. Osa stared at the impala group she and Pomeroy obtained. "[E]very mounted animal," they saw "meant an adventure."

When they reached the gorilla group, they forgot their chilled night on top of Mount Mikeno. "We saw only that marvelous view," explained Martin, "so real and so colorful. . . . Some, who do not know Africa, will think the colorings are exaggerated, but we know they are not." Akeley would be glad, they thought, at the completion of his vision. Now "the people of America could see Africa exactly as it is—Africa that will some day disappear as civilization marches in." The thought of being part of this filled them with pride.

In New York they worked on the feature film, then toured with a lecture film, *Wonders of the Congo*. The feature, *Congorilla*, was the hit, however. It thrilled audiences with some of the best footage of gorillas in their natural habitat—in pictures and sound. The film had its world premiere at the Winter Garden in New York City on July 21, 1932. "The First and Only Talking

Around the world, advertisements for *Congorilla* portrayed gorillas as exceedingly ferocious beasts, despite the film's rather tame specimens.

Picture Made Entirely in Africa," announced one ad, promising "Those Intrepid Adventurers from Kansas take you with them on their jungle safari." Other ads for *Congorilla* drew people in with exaggerated illustrations of ferocious-looking beasts. While this was the very myth the Johnsons were trying to debunk, they went along with such promotion. The film itself showed rather docile gorillas, save the anxious screams of the two they captured.

The Johnsons were again breaking new ground by bridging the gap between science and popular culture. They lured audiences in with advertisements promising savage-looking beasts, then treated them to scenes of gorillas that undermined the popular imagery. By doing so, the Johnsons ensured success of their film while inserting a subtle conservation message: These animals were at home in the wilderness and should be left unmolested. Even the scenes of gorilla capture reinforced this message in the screams of the ensnared gorillas. They wanted to be left alone, to live their peaceful lives in the forest. Only human contact made them "wild."

CHAPTER 5

SAFARI SKIES

Had I been told, three years ago, that on our next expedition to Africa we would fly our own airplanes for 60,000 miles over the jungles and lakes and plains of the once "dark" continent, I would have been convinced that my informant was mad.

— MARTIN JOHNSON

Mountains, jungle, plain were a vast panorama beneath us; great elephant migrations, herds of thousands, also great flocks of white herons and countless giraffe and plains game . . .

— OSA JOHNSON

While in New York in early 1932, the Johnsons got word that Martin's father, John, was sick, so they flew to Kansas despite Martin's "definite and deep-seated aversion to flying." Their travels thus far had been by boat, train, or car; airplanes had not yet figured into their modes of transportation. After this uneventful flight to Kansas, however, Martin wondered about the possibilities of planes in Africa. What wonderful things you could see flying above the herds of the plains and over rugged mountaintops, he thought. When Osa awoke the next morning, Martin was gone. He had returned to the airport to talk with its manager, Vern Carstens, about flying lessons. Osa's father teased her, "If you're going to keep up with Martin this time, you'll have to grow yourself a pair of wings."

While roads and the use of automobiles made many parts of Africa more accessible than before, some landscape features were not easily traversed by car. Flooded rivers controlled seasonal movements. Mud, swamps, sand, and steep, rocky terrain limited car travel, especially without porters willing to pull or carry vehicles through rough spots. "[M]otor cars are utterly useless," realized Martin, "when some new and fascinating region beckoned."

Carstens took the two adventurers on as students, teaching them how to fly and how to navigate by air. Osa's first solo flight was something of a disaster; she was certainly not an Amelia Earhart, the fellow Kansan who had piloted across the Atlantic Ocean in 1928. Her whole family had come to watch, though her mother and father did not look pleased with her new hobby, which seemed too full of daring for their little girl. Her more adventuresome grandmother Minnie, however, glowed with pride. Osa flew up two thousand feet and glided just fine—it was landing that was the trick. She tried once and bounced off the ground several times. On the fourth try, she landed. Though Carstens reprimanded her for being too close to the trees and telephone wires, Osa felt proud. While the Johnsons did not, as Martin put it, attain "any Lindberghian ability as pilots," they became comfortable enough with the controls that they began dreaming of photographing Africa by air—and exploring remote regions inaccessible by land travel.

Back East, Martin and Osa went to visit the Sikorsky plant in Bridgeport, Connecticut. Though they claimed they had no intentions of investing in aircraft at that time, they left the plant

Martin and Osa were thrilled with the ease their Sikorskys brought to their African safari.

as owners of two amphibious planes. On a whim they ordered custom paint jobs: The one they named *Osa's Ark* had zebra stripes, and the other, *Spirit of Africa*, was painted to resemble a giraffe hide.

The insides were custom made to meet their safari needs. The seats were taken out to make room for their camera equipment, and sleeping bunks, a washroom, and a gas stove were installed, along with a camera that could be used while in flight. Osa designed a typewriter desk at which she could continue writing. Her *Jungle Babies* stories, telling amusing and heartwarming anecdotes about her pet wild animals, were a hit, and she had taken on more book and magazine projects.

Since they still had much to learn about actually flying in the field, the Johnsons hired Carstens to go with them to Africa. They also hired another pilot, Boris Sergievsky, and Al Morway, a mechanic who knew Sikorskys well. Two soundmen, Arthur Sanial and Robert Moreno, and a photography assistant, Hugh Davis, rounded out the crew. As they added all this new technology to their expedition, Martin lamented, knowing he would have even less time now for taking still photographs. "I get a great deal more pleasure," he said, in the artistry of those.

They sailed from New York to Cape Town, deciding to approach Nairobi from the south for the first time. The planes they had packed and shipped were unloaded and assembled, and Sergievsky and Carstens tested them out before they began the 4,400 miles to Nairobi. Flying over mountains and through fogs, they found their maps were inaccurate, and there were few fields or bodies of water on which they could land. Towns were farther apart than they had calculated. They needed to make frequent stops to refuel as their tanks lasted only five hours.

They made it halfway, to a town called Broken Hill, without incident. From there they calculated the next stop, Mpika, would be only a three-hour flight. After four hours of flying, however, they still did not see the town. Below them were mountains and streams full of rocks—there was nowhere to land. Martin and Osa flew with Sergievsky, but Carstens had fallen far behind. Their tank was about to hit empty, and Osa frantically scanned the landscape with binoculars for a place to land. To her relief, she saw a lake just six miles away. Sergievsky turned and landed on the surface in the nick of time.

They had landed on the private lake of Lt. Col. Stewart Gore-Brown, retired, and his wife. Their mansion was fronted by an expansive lawn in the midst of a coffee plantation that contrasted with the surrounding jungle. The Gore-Browns, quite amused to have the famous adventurers land so suddenly on their lake, supplied them with gas and directions to Mpika. The Johnsons had, they discovered, gone too far and flown right over the town. Carstens, whom they were so worried about, had landed there safely.

They continued to Nairobi, where their soundmen, who had gone ahead by land, had cleared an airfield on which they could land. Osa aired out their home and bought supplies for their safari while Martin and the men cleaned and tested all the camera and

The *Spirit of Africa* flies above a herd of elephants. This photograph, taken from *Osa's Ark*, shows the unique views Osa and Martin now enjoyed.

sound equipment. After two months of preparations, they set off.

Martin and Osa felt a new freedom with the Sikorsky planes. "Mountains, jungle, plain were a vast panorama beneath us," commented Osa, "great elephant migrations, herds of thousands, also great flocks of white herons and countless giraffe and plains game were spotted one moment from the air, and the next moment were being recorded by our cameras." They flew over Lake Paradise and marveled at the hundreds of miles of wilderness sanctuary in which they had once lived.

Their first stop was at Lake Rudolf (now Lake Turkana), a "curious and desolate body of salt water" on the border of Kenya and Abyssinia (now Ethiopia). The barren lake stretched for nearly two hundred miles, surrounded by "stunted trees" and "hot, fierce, unending winds." Martin wanted to go to an island in the southern portion of the lake where he had heard a group of people, known as Elmolos, lived, who knew nothing of the rest of the world. When they arrived, however, Carstens said the water was too rough to land. Through binoculars, the Johnsons could see the choppy waters and knew he was right. They tried again and again, but always the lake was too rough.

So they flew farther north over Center Island and three crater lakes where Carstens saw a sandy beach. He set the plane down there, and Martin and Osa took their cameras to one of the lakes, where they had seen an abundance of birdlife from the plane. Hundreds of herons populated the lake, as well as numerous crocodiles. Martin and Osa disagreed about its beauty. Martin thought it would be a great place to live, but Osa thought the barrenness and the burning sun were "horrid." The wind was picking up, so Carstens called them back to the beach, but even though they hurried, they took off in dangerously high waves. Intrigued by the spot, Martin wanted to return. "The scenery," he said, "had all the qualities of a surrealist painting."

Now that they were able to reach little-explored areas of the country, Martin and Osa found natives who were puzzled by their white skin. In a cove on Lake Rudolf, they met members of the Turkana people, who had long hair "plastered with mud and tallow and molded into the most ingenious forms." Their hair was exceptionally thick, as they added the hair of their dead relatives to their own sculpted masses "of such bizarre design and abstract quality as would delight a sculptor of the modern school." Their noses and lips were pierced and held wooden or ivory disks, and their bodies were covered in mud and alkali.

The Turkana's striking appearance was something Martin and Osa had to get on film. As Carstens repositioned the plane, Osa and Martin watched the people for their reaction, but they seemed unfazed and unimpressed. In fact, the Turkana's favorite thing about the planes was the shade provided by their wings.

This startled the Johnsons, as the native men they had hired as assistants refused to enter the planes, preferring to walk hundreds of miles. It was not out of superstition, Martin supposed, but because they had seen motors on cars fail and did not want to be thousands of feet above the ground if the plane's motor should do the same.

Seeing the Turkana were unafraid, Martin took some of the people up in his plane. Their perceptions of the landscape were much different than his. When Martin pointed out a cow on the ground, the Turkana insisted he was wrong. "A cow has legs," they replied, and from this angle, they could see none. Nor was a tree a tree. "You look up to see a tree," they replied, "and you can walk under a tree. That is not a tree."

When they returned to Nairobi, Martin and Osa received word from F. Trubee Davison, president of the American Museum of Natural History, that he and his wife, Dot, were in town and planning to collect the last elephants for the African Hall. Although the Davisons had a U.S. Army pilot with them, Pete Quesada, Trubee had never been to Africa and wanted to see it by land. The Johnsons, Quesada, and Dot flew to Garissa, where they met Davison to hunt for elephants along the Tana River—Kenya's longest.

While they stayed some days with the Davisons, Martin and Osa were most interested in obtaining aerial shots of elephant herds. When the hunters had gathered four specimens for the museum, the Johnsons took them to see Tanganyika—Akeley's lion den. They set up camp, then flew farther over the plains, thinking the curious lions that had loved to try to play with their cars would be quite intrigued by the giant machine.

Martin set up the cameras, and Osa stayed in the plane. When a lion came nearby, growling, Osa lifted the hatch and called to him to be quiet. She saw Martin, alarmed, watching her from his camera and quickly closed the hatch. The lion, however, pounced toward her, landing on the glass. Hamming it up for the camera, Osa threw a bag of flour at the lion. It comically covered his head

Osa watches a lion pride from the safety of *Osa's Ark*'s cabin.

and nose in a fluff of white powder. The lion walked away, "bewildered and enraged," described Osa.

The protection and transportation provided by the Sikorskys increased the Johnsons' enjoyment of these safaris. "We are having the time of our young lives with our airplanes," reported Martin excitedly, praising their comfort and time-saving aspects. They also made for more "thrills," he said, as they could come closer to wildlife but remain inside the plane's resilient walls. Osa loved them now, too, as she could go fishing in any spot she liked, whenever she liked. They simply landed on a lake, spent the day fishing, then cooked and slept right on board the plane. Now that hundreds of porters were no longer necessary, Martin and Osa felt liberated. "Gosh! It is wonderful to be free," rejoiced Martin, "no laws or rules to obey . . . we are just a couple of African tramps having the best time we have ever had."

Not wishing to relive their ill-fated climb up Mount Kenya, they flew around it, and Martin finally got his long-desired pictures

Martin, Osa, and their crew picnic in the Sikorsky's shade displaying a box of Bisquick, possibly meant for an advertisement or endorsement.

of its icy peak. They thrilled at the experience of flying so close to the mountain. Fields of wildflowers were blurs of bright colors. They saw the bamboo forest through which they had hiked, and the forest sloping down to the plains. Martin couldn't wait to show audiences the footage "of those majestic pinnacles of almost terrifying beauty."

Martin and Osa returned to the Northern Frontier, adding aerial photography and sound to scenes they had filmed before. At a stream running between two cliffs, Martin set up his camera on top of one of the cliffs, positioning more cameras and sound equipment a half mile below. As soon as everything was set up, a normally nocturnal leopard appeared down below in the bright rays of the sun. Martin cranked the camera and then told his assistants to scare the animal up. Upon hearing the men, the leopard bared its teeth and leaped up toward the top of the cliff—and Martin. But the cat did not make it; it slipped and slid down the cliff, making for a great picture and ensuring Martin's safety.

Next they flew over the gorilla country of the Belgian Congo and the Ituri Forest, which was home of the pygmy people they had met on their previous expedition. They landed to visit the friendly Mbuti and see their reaction to the aircraft. After much encouragement, they piled thirty-six of the braver ones into one plane. They who sang for the entire ride, just as they had done when they rode in the Willys-Knights. The airborne Mbuti looked down and pointed enthusiastically at things they recognized on the ground. They were most impressed with the plane's speed. Upon reaching a familiar gathering hill, they were awestruck—they had only traveled for twenty minutes to this place, which took them two days to walk to.

On another flight Osa and Martin took the teenage daughters of the chief. When they landed, the chief's wife ran tearfully to her girls, kissing them, glad they were unscathed. This was the first time, Osa reflected, in all their years exploring, that they had seen any natives kiss one another. "Never before . . . had I seen such obvious signs of affection," said Osa. "[M]other love among the pygmies of the Ituri is no different from the mother love to which we have grown accustomed to [in America]," she confided.

On their way back to Nairobi, Osa began to have unusual vaginal bleeding. When they arrived there, she stayed with a nurse while Martin completed a flight around Mount Kilimanjaro. Carstens said it was too high to fly over—some two thousand feet higher than Mount Kenya—but agreed to circle the mountain instead so Martin could photograph its snow-capped peak for the first time. Then they outfitted one plane with a bed for Osa, where she lay as they began their return to London through Tororo, Juba, Malakel, and Khartoum. Elephants by the thousands dotted the plains below, and Martin made Carstens fly low so he could get pictures. They retraced the slow boat ride they took with Eastman and saw the great Egyptian ruins in the Valley of the Kings and Cairo from above.

They flew over the North African colonies belonging to Italy and France, stopping in Bengasi, Tripoli, Tunis, the Mediterranean,

Sardinia, Cannes, Lyons, Paris, and over the channel to London. They stayed in London for six days, then loaded the planes and themselves onto the S.S. *Manhattan,* bound for New York. Their Sikorskys had taken them, Osa estimated, over sixty thousand miles of African jungles and beyond.

"It is the most wonderful sensation to fly away to unknown parts," said Martin, "see the wonder of the savages as we land, watch elephants and rhino and buffalo from the air and photograph them." *Osa's Ark,* he confided, was correctly named. His wife had collected numerous pets on their travels—lions, cheetahs, porcupines, bush babies, mongooses, wild fowl, and more than sixty monkeys. Osa particularly loved her four little cheetahs, who made themselves at home on her bed and showed their affection by licking her neck. "We tame [the pets] and at night always have a few around the table eating with us," revealed Martin. "I suppose we are a little crazy, but if so it is fun to be crazy."

On August 9, 1934, Martin and Osa arrived back in New York, and they again found themselves the center of attention. A young illustrator wrote to Martin to tell him he wanted to put their adventures in the papers, not as news stories, but in a new medium—the comic strip. Martin also had other opportunities in the works—he talked with five-and-ten-cent stores to see if they would release books and painting sets showing the animals the Johnsons had encountered on their adventures, and he had the idea to start a Martin Johnson Kodak Club for young fans. He invented a camera, which he called the Martin Johnson Aerial Camera, and hoped Kodak would manufacture it.

However, things were not all positive. Osa addressed her recent illness and underwent surgery for a uterine tumor. Her mother had come to be with her, but shortly after her operation word came from Kansas that her father had been killed in a freak train accident. Her mother and Martin left Osa to recover alone and flew to Chanute.

Osa's inspirations for her jungle pet stories stay close at hand while she attempts to type.

Throughout the fall of 1934, Martin and Osa worked on *Baboona,* their commercial film for Fox, and a lecture film they called *Wings Over Africa.* The last expedition all but bankrupted them, costing more than $160,000, and they hoped the film would at the very least earn them their money back. At the end of the year, *Baboona* premiered, suitably, on board an airplane. The publicity stunt recruited daring pilot Eddie Rickenbacker to fly from New York to Miami, round-trip, in the fastest time recorded. When the film premiered for the general public in New York in January 1935, it was at a grand gala attended by museum dignitaries and wealthy socialites, including Walter Chrysler, Bayard Colgate, and Richard Mellon.

The Johnsons were more popular than ever, especially with children. They received countless letters from young fans asking for autographs and, sometimes, if they could come with them on their next adventure. The Johnsons were also recruited to endorse Coca-Cola. In one advertisement Osa stood with the beverage in front of her zebra-striped plane. In another Martin was quoted: "There's nothing so invigorating as Coca-Cola on our long, hot safaris . . . Believe me, it helps make life worth living out here." They could not escape media attention. One of the animals they transported back from Africa, a baby elephant named Toto Tembo, was flown to the St. Louis Zoo, with newsreels and newspaper articles featuring Osa dropping off the twenty-week-old pachyderm. One paper called Osa "A Modern Diana" after the Greek goddess of the hunt.

Though their films had made them icons of adventure, the Johnsons were slowing down. Osa was now forty-one years old and perhaps worried about another traumatic illness striking her in the field. Osa told Martin she only wanted to go on short expeditions from then on, and he seemed content with the idea. Having spent so much time filming in Africa, they felt they had done about all they could to bring that continent's rumored "dark" landscape to light. They had destroyed myths about the native people and the ferocity of African animals. Now they decided to return to another familiar landscape—Borneo. Their adventures had come full circle.

In August 1935 Martin and Osa boarded a ship for British North Borneo (now Sabah). They planned to revisit the jungles where they had previously had such a difficult time photographing wildlife and, with their two Sikorsky planes, *Osa's Ark* and the newly renamed *Spirit of Africa and Borneo* (which had gained a painted eye on its bow—a Chinese and Arabic tradition meant to ward off evil spirits), hoped to explore more of the country. Sound was again a crucial addition to their previous films. To assist them were pilot Jim Laneri and soundman Joe Tilton.

They sailed across the Mediterranean and Indian Oceans to

Sumatra. Martin, Osa, and Laneri disembarked there with one plane and sent Tilton by boat to Singapore. Laneri flew the plane to Kuala Lumpur, then to Singapore, where they mingled and dined with the Sultan of Johore. Escorted by a British Royal Air Force plane, they completed the flight to Kuching. They planned to take a flight path around the coast of Borneo, but at the last minute adventure beckoned. The coastal route was well known, and the Johnsons wanted something better. Few had piloted over Borneo's rugged interior, so they set to explore that route instead.

They flew from Labuan above the Paper River, following its route toward its headwaters in the Crocker Mountains. Their clear views were abruptly taken away by a fast-moving storm that had them flying blindly through clouds and driving rain. The sky cleared just long enough for them to spot Mount Kinabalu, Borneo's tallest peak, before another storm surrounded them. Not knowing if they'd make it to their next fuel supply, the frustrated crew turned around and landed exactly where they had begun, at Labuan.

Fearing the inland Borneo skies, the Johnsons reluctantly switched back to the coastal route. They made it as far as Kimanis Bay before a particularly clear day tempted them to try again. This time no storms got in their way. They flew over the mountains, next to Mount Kinabalu, and made it to the eastern coast of Borneo, facing the Sulu Sea. They landed at Sandakan and were greeted as guests of the governor, who lent them a house on the hilltop overlooking the sea. Martin and Osa made their base there, taking a few short trips around Sandakan Bay and preparing for their expedition to the interior.

When they were ready, they returned to the Kinabatangan River, hiring porters, guides, an interpreter, gobongs, and a Chinese junk. For their camp they cleared a large swath of land and erected a total of twenty buildings, including a lab and an airplane hangar. Because of the soft ground that flooded during storms, they had raised walkways built all around the village.

As they had done at Lake Paradise, they plastered the inside walls of their home and attempted to decorate with what materials they had on hand. The floor of their bedroom was made from the crates in which they had transported their food, and Osa laughed at the absurdity of being surrounded by labels for Bartlett pears, Heinz Tomato Ketchup, Mammoth white asparagus, Old Dutch Cleanser, Bon Ami, and California prunes. As she was wont to do, Osa attempted to plant a garden with seeds from home, but the animals there were worse than in Africa. Everything she planted was stolen or ruined by pestering monkeys. She enjoyed preparing dinners for the men and setting a formal table with a vase of wild orchids at its center, and once she even cooked up a "home-styled American dinner" for the crew with a turkey, cranberry sauce, sweet potatoes, creamed onions, asparagus, peas, and stuffing. Such things were, she believed, "a little spark of comfort in an otherwise black void of hardship and privation."

Transferring that notion of comfort to their river trip, Martin and Osa prepared a gobong to suit them. It had several separate areas—bedroom, darkroom, kitchen, and storage. There was even a refrigerator on board, and the whole raft was equipped with electric lights. But these comforts did not distract them from the jungle outside. As they floated along the Kinabatangan River, Martin and Osa were amazed by the forests of the interior. It was, described Osa, a "riotous range of green." The forest was denser than they had remembered and filled with wildlife that their cameras could not capture years ago. Monkeys were everywhere, as were snakes. The juxtapositions awed Osa. She found the beauty of the forest's butterflies and the hideousness of its leeches difficult to reconcile.

Other animals were more difficult to find, but Martin and Osa successfully shot rare film of elusive sun bears, flying foxes, and maroon leaf monkeys. The star of the expedition—and of the commercial film they would release—was the proboscis monkey. The rare, bulging-nosed animal had never been captured on film

The comforts of their houseboat on the Kinabatangan River included a refrigerator and trays of ice cubes, which Osa offers to a native girl.

in the wild and was difficult to keep alive in captivity. The Johnsons also encountered both stampeding and docile elephants, wondering again at the contrasts of nature, apparent even within the same species.

Martin and Osa captured the sound of native dances and ceremonies, but the highlight of the film was the capture of a three-hundred-pound orangutan. They used the same method in which they had captured the gorillas in the Congo—scare the ape up a tree, then force it down into an enclosed area. But the full-grown orangutan was more stubborn than the young gorillas had been. He stayed in the tree for three days, ignoring and scowling at their attempts to get him down. Even swooping above him in the Sikorsky produced no results.

When he grew hungry enough to take a risk, the orangutan scampered down the tree and tried to escape into the forest, but Martin's men were waiting with a net and quickly trapped the

Osa grooming one of the orangutan they captured in Borneo.

animal. In a stunt seemingly pulled from Merian Cooper's *King Kong* (1933), they introduced Truson, as they named him, to the American public in a cage at the American Museum of Natural History. At the time he was the largest orangutan to ever be held in captivity. Martin and Osa gave Truson to the Bronx Zoo and gave another orangutan they had captured, named Bujang, to the San Diego Zoo.

After fourteen months in Borneo, Martin and Osa were glad to be back in New York. Martin edited their film and worked in his office at the museum. He completed their lecture film *Jungle Depths of Borneo* and began work on the sound film *Borneo,* which was printed on sepia film that made the mountains, ocean, and jungles of the South Seas glow like never before. "The explorer in Martin had long ago been satisfied," wrote one raving critic, "the artist, until now, had not."

Martin and Osa found the lecture circuit had grown considerably since they first began touring. Though they had taken care of their own affairs thus far, they now found it necessary to hire an agent to arrange their bookings. In the fall of 1936, they signed with Clark Getts, who managed radio and lecture appearances and promoted the Johnsons as "Speakers Who Can Speak." He booked a full tour for their Borneo lecture, stopping first in Salt Lake City.

"The beauty of Borneo we could not capture with the cameras of those days," Martin explained to the audience assembled at the Mormon Tabernacle in Salt Lake City, as he referred to their first expedition to the island in 1920, "and so you see . . . we had to go back." As the film rolled behind him, Martin told the crowd of nine thousand children about the forests and mountains of Borneo, their jungle camp, and the hundreds of animals and flowers they encountered every day. The audience responded positively to Martin's casual demeanor, expressing awe at the landscape, laughing at the odd proboscis monkeys, cooing at the cute sun bear, and recoiling at descriptions of bugs and snakes. At the end, Martin took Osa's hand, and they bowed to endless applause.

Energized by the enthralled audience, Osa and Martin left Salt Lake City and headed to California, to visit the ape they had collected for the San Diego Zoological Park. As the commercial flight from Salt Lake City to Los Angeles neared its destination, a dense fog moved into the San Fernando Valley, and the pilot lost his way. Just east of the Burbank Airport, the plane smacked into the side of a mountain.

Knowing the famous adventurers were on board, the media rushed to the scene. People around the country sat on the edge of their seats to listen to the live radio broadcast and learn Martin and Osa's fate. In the background the distressed screams and moan of one man in particular could be heard, and it was feared that this was Martin Johnson. This was confirmed the next morning, when his death was announced over the radio waves across the country.

"The jungles are really safe when you know how to get along in them," Martin had remarked in his last interview. "America, probably because it is the most civilized place in the world, is the most dangerous." Throughout his life, Martin had commented on the dangers of so-called civilization, praising the wilderness and seeking its comforts. He had faced all manner of wild dangers and come away unscathed. Now the public who had grown to love him and his intrepid wife, who had survived, was left to make sense of his tragic death.

CHAPTER 6

Osa Alone

I have had the right sort of woman to take along with me into the desert and jungle. If ever a man needed a partner in his chosen profession, it has been I. And if ever a wife were a partner to a man, it is Osa Johnson.

—MARTIN JOHNSON

We had only our hopes and our nerve . . .Nothing is impossible, if you want it badly enough, and if you have the imagination to dream and the energy to make your dreams come true.

—OSA JOHNSON

"It is an ironic twist of fate that we do not often die from the main hazards of our calling, but by the incidental mischances along the byways of peace," posited one reporter struggling to make sense of the senseless death of Martin Johnson. This man, who had lived among carnivores and cannibals, who had risked his safety for nearly his entire life, had died at the age of fifty-seven in a crash of a routine commercial flight from Salt Lake City to Los Angeles. According to friends, Osa was distraught. Her former nurse in Nairobi told an interviewer she received a letter from Osa after Martin's death: "Osa was heartbroken, as they deeply loved each other. There was such a happy atmosphere around them." But Osa, who had survived the crash with injuries, was ever aware of her public image. From her hospital bed she rallied enough courage to tell her fans she would never stop exploring. "I was scared when we first started these expeditions," she admitted. "I guess most women would be. But now—I love it. I can't wait to get back in the jungles."

On May 28, 1937, four and a half months after the crash, Osa rolled her wheelchair onto the stage at Constitution Hall in Washington, D.C., to introduce *Jungle Depths of Borneo*—the last film she and Martin had made together. Her fractured leg was still too weak for her to stand on, though she had left the hospital nearly three months before. With her was soundman Joe Tilton, who had carried on with most of the Johnsons' planned lecture tour. Though Osa had been well enough to join him in March, their agent, Clark Getts, had trouble booking her alone, so they had to wait until May. Theater managers were resistant to a female headliner, thinking it would not bring in enough of a crowd. Some even insisted she be listed as Mrs. Martin Johnson, rather than Osa. This sexism made Osa bristle; she began to realize that perhaps the world did not appreciate her part in the adventures she had shared with Martin.

In finishing the Borneo lecture tour she had started with Martin, Osa felt she was fulfilling their shared mission to lift "the veil on this exotic and unexplored land for the first time." After his death, his colleagues praised Martin's contributions to science and film. American Museum of Natural History president F. Trubee Davison praised him as "a naturalist and explorer of exceptional courage and experience," and the Explorers Club sent an official condolence (but not an invitation for membership) to

Osa dedicates her time to teaching children about wildlife in AMNH's African Hall.

Osa mourning the loss of "a great soul, a lovable personality and a tremendous force." But beyond the loss of a man of "science, exploration, and education," friends and acquaintances mourned the loss of the charming, adventuresome couple. "The partnership of Martin and Osa has been broken in the only way that it could have been destroyed," lamented museum colleague Roy Chapman Andrews. "Osa is left alone to carry on the work which they both loved. Only she can know what courage it takes to do what she is doing."

The lecture in Washington was organized by the Child Welfare League of America, and all proceeds went to the charity. In her life after Martin, Osa spent more time helping charities for children. She began to combine her love of wild places and longing for children of her own through her tales and toys. So her pets could be admired by the city's children, she rented her domesticated cheetahs to the California Zoological Society's Zoopark in Los Angeles, and she gave permission for them to be rented out to movie studios.

Osa also lent her support to several wildlife conservation organizations. The animals from her children's stories were made into stuffed toys endorsed by the National Wildlife Foundation, and Osa Johnson's Pets were featured in the front window display at New York's FAO Schwartz. A member of the American Museum of Natural History, the Society of Women Geographers, the National Wildlife Federation, the Girl Scouts of America, and the Adventurer's Club, she was named honorary chairman of the National Wildlife Federation Week (along with actor-singer Bing Crosby and Secretary of the Interior Oscar L. Chapman) to honor the role of women in conservation.

At a tree-planting ceremony at the Dawes Arboretum in Columbus, Ohio, in November 1940, Osa spoke about the direction she hoped her life would take. "[S]ince my heart is in Africa and I am giving you an African tree, I feel that I am leaving part of my heart here," she said as she broke ground. "I have resolved to spend the rest of my own life trying to make people happy, not only with motion pictures and entertainment, but by easing the pressure that makes misery and tension and misunderstanding," she continued. "Lives like trees can be made strong and beautiful if they are given a little attention and encouragement."

Garnering the support of her wealthy and charitable friends, including George Dryden and Perry Osborn (acting president of the American Museum of Natural History and the son of Henry Fairfield Osborn, former president of the museum), Osa began

In a promotional photograph, Osa holds one of her National Wildlife Federation– endorsed Jungle Pets, Twiga the Giraffe.

to form her own charity for children. Although the charity never seemed to have coalesced, this work was part of her new definition of herself. "When my life was spared in our plane accident," she wrote in a letter to Kansas senator Capper, looking for his support, "I wondered for what purpose. But as I talk to thousands of happy children and receive their appreciative letters about my film, books and stories, and their requests for advice, I feel that I have found the purpose. I am devoting my life to them. I understand them and I feel that they can be inspired to fine private lives and great public work if they have the right influence and are shown their opportunities in this amazing country of ours. You and I made our dreams come true, but others have to be encouraged to do so."

Because she had spent so much time in wild places, Osa was an anomaly in America. Not only was she a woman who hunted, she was a fashionable woman who hunted. In March 1939 the *New York Times* announced the Fashion Academy's picks for the best-dressed women. Among the twelve winners chosen at a ceremony at the Waldorf Astoria were actress Bette Davis, millionaire wife Mrs. Alfred Vanderbilt, and Osa Johnson. She was cited for her "scientific knowledge of jungle attire in everyday fashion."

In addition to her other endeavors, Osa founded her own line of clothing, which she called Osafari. The clothing was meant as luxury sportswear, made with durable fabrics and wooden buttons. The key to her line, however, were colors inspired by Africa, including Maasai Bronze, Kenya Blue, and Uganda Flame. One popular item was her Congo Glove. "Whether on safari or on Fifth Avenue," her ad read, "the first lady of exploration puts her name behind this smart, cleanly designed glove." While Osa was known for wearing furs and hides (a pair of zebra-hide shoes were among the most unusual of her items), she quickly quieted the comments of those who thought such attire was cruel. "Whenever we kill a bustard we always save the wings for a hat," she explained, regarding her hunting as a form of thrift inherited from her pioneer grandmother. Thus, according to Osa it was not in conflict with her conservation, but a part of it.

Osa's other claim to fame, an unusual sort of naturalistic safari cuisine, also earned her accolades and attention in the United States. Her recipes for Roast Eland and Guinea Fowl à la King were published in a compilation of sportsmen's memoirs. *Cosmopolitan* ran a full article by Osa telling readers "what and how to eat in the wilds." Her recipe for Gazelle Consommé appeared in a promotion for the Johnsons' comic strip, *Danger Trails,* which by that time was running in several newspapers across the country. "The point about Gazelle Consommé," began the recipe, "is to first catch your gazelle. Then, having caught him, to make soup out of him. It is almost impossible, to bring yourself to the soup point when gazing into his large, soft, limpid eyes that beg you to open up a can of soup instead!"

Osa wanted to continue photographing, filming, and writing, as she had done by Martin's side, and she planned a return trip to Africa. But when the Second World War spread into North Africa in the summer of 1940, she cancelled her trip. Osa returned to Africa just once after Martin's death, as consultant for the film *Stanley & Livingstone* (1939). The film traced reporter Henry Stanley's search for missionary David Livingstone, who had gone missing in the jungles of the African Congo. With her expertise on filming and managing safaris, Osa was a perfect adviser to assist with scenes shot in Africa. She sailed in June with her agent, Clark Getts, who was quickly becoming more Osa's companion than manager. Director Otto Brower was in Kenya shooting on-location shots for the film, and Osa advised him on scenery, guided him to spots she thought would work for certain scenes, and helped assemble natives for filming. She also showed him techniques for filming wildlife and managed the safari camp. During their three months in Africa, Getts marveled at her comfort in the field: "She was at her best then and had no equal." Despite disapproving letters and comments about their affair, Osa and Getts were secretly married in April 1940 at George Eastman's North Carolina retreat.

Osa, who had written several articles about the state of African wildlife for the *New York Times* on this last trip, now set out to write her own version of her life with Martin. While she sometimes used ghost writers, the experiences and story ideas were all hers. She published two books on her adventures with Martin— *I Married Adventure* (1939) and *Four Years in Paradise* (1941). The distinctive zebra-striped cover of *I Married Adventure* made it an instant classic, and the narrative inside earned it a spot on the *New York Times* best-seller list for several weeks. The book became a film, starring Osa herself and using clips drawn from their years of safari filming, but it was not a hit with reviewers. Despite years in front of cameras and her naturally charming public persona, Osa had little talent for acting. Nonetheless, the public's love for the Johnsons packed theaters. Osa capitalized on this interest and wrote several children's books, based on her pets, including *Osa Johnson's Jungle Friends* (1939), *Pantaloons* (1941), and *Snowball* (1942), which were hits.

In 1946 her marriage to Getts hit rocky ground. Accusing her of alcoholism, Getts placed Osa in a Connecticut psychiatric sanitarium, where she remained for a few months. When she was discharged, she did not return to Getts, filing for an annulment, accusing him of embezzling money from her company and hiding his imprisonment for being a conscientious objector during World War I. He in turn accused her of violent drunken outbursts. The arguing continued for years until Osa filed for, and won, a divorce in 1949. "I have had many difficulties to overcome of late (much more difficult and menacing than even our African rhinos!)," she confided to a friend, "all I can say is that there are sometimes more hazards in living among so-called civilized people than living in the jungles among savages and wild animals!" After formally divorcing Getts, Osa earned a contract with a television producer (a task Getts failed to do, blaming her drunken episodes) for her very own television program. Osa Johnson's *Big Game Hunt* ran for twenty-six episodes and featured Osa talking about her travels with Martin and the habits of wild animals. Osa's series was among the first nature shows made for television and appealed to children and adults with its playful narration of animal antics. Whatever her troubles, Osa was still doing what she loved and was even talking about another trip to Africa—this time for color pictures.

Some say Osa eventually lost the television contract because of her drinking, but to reduce Osa to a depressed alcoholic at the end of her life discredits all that she accomplished. Here was a working woman in an era when such a thing was barely respectable. To lose the partner with whom she shared everything from the time she was sixteen years old was not only an emotional tragedy, it also could have been the end of her career and her ability to support herself. Getts may have had trouble booking Osa for lectures on her own, but it would have been nearly impossible for her to succeed in the business without him. Clinging to him as she did so shortly after Martin's death indicates she saw this as a business relationship, not an emotional one. Having lost her first love, she was likely not prepared for another.

When the dissatisfaction of her new marriage set in, Osa, as a woman, had limited options. She indicated to a friend that she knew Getts was embezzling money from her for years but didn't feel that she could do anything about it. Even when she filed for an annulment, it took more than three years, and a separate divorce filing, to earn her independence. As time went on, she was involved in another problematic relationship. In the early 1950s Osa was living with her lawyer, John Crane, whom she knew to be a degenerate gambler. He had sold a valuable jade necklace of hers and lied about its value to support his habit. This choice of companions is more difficult to reconcile. Throughout her life Osa seemed a strong, independent woman, but after Martin's death, that spirit seems to have waned.

While Osa may have had emotional scars, they certainly did not keep her from her ambitions. Between Martin's death and her own, Osa produced seven books, several articles, two lecture films, and a TV show, and she appeared throughout the country as a leading act—finally able to hold her own as both a female headliner and as Osa Johnson (not just Mrs. Martin Johnson). She wrote in support of wildlife conservation and instilled an affection for wild animals in the next generation of Americans. Though her travels took her around the world, Osa's—and Martin's—true contribution was in bringing wild places home to America.

On January 7, 1953, Crane found Osa dead in her bathtub in her New York City apartment. She had suffered a heart attack

On her lecture tour, "African Paradise," Osa finally earned billing under her own name, rather than as "Mrs. Martin Johnson."

and fallen where she stood. In the months previous, doctors had treated her for both hypertension and coronary artery disease. Crane claimed they had been planning an African safari and she had simply worn herself out. For years Osa had maintained she had a safari "in the works." She died as she had lived—dreaming of adventure.

"And a lion skin, after all," wrote Martin in 1934, "is no such trophy as a thousand feet of close-up motion picture film." While Osa's hunting trophies were largely auctioned off after her death, or sold by herself toward the end of her life, it is the Johnsons' books and films that endure. Osa's impala remains on display in the American Museum of Natural History's Akeley Hall of African Mammals, and a small plaque nearby mentions her participation in collecting specimens for the diorama. After her death, her mother, Clark Getts, and several former safari mates and friends organized to create a museum to honor the Johnsons' legacy. The Martin and Osa Johnson Safari Museum is in Chanute, Kansas, the same town where Osa was born. It is an unlikely place to house the legacy of these world travelers, but since Chanute was the hometown Osa and Martin so often returned to, even after their adventures and celebrity might have kept them away, it seems a fitting locale for such a memorial.

"People remember Martin and Osa Johnson most for their movies of Africa, Borneo, and the South Seas," says museum director Conrad Froehlich. "Although this work may represent an outmoded genre of travel-adventure films, the Johnsons' legacy— remaining in thousands of photographs, hundreds of cans of motion picture film footage, and numerous books and articles— remains an invaluable contribution to our knowledge of some of the world's most beautiful, and mysterious, places." These films, photographs, and writings, however, are not mere relics of the past; they remain important records of landscapes, peoples, and animals that have changed irrevocably over the past decades. Anthropologists have watched the Johnsons' films to learn about rituals, adornments, and dances of cultures that have lost their traditions. The people of Malayasia have embraced photographs of the region and their ancestors in a partnership between the Safari Museum and the Sabah Museum, which opened an exhibit of Johnson photographs in 2010 at the Sandakan Heritage Center. Wildlife biologists compare the enormity of wildlife herds

Osa and Martin shared their love of adventure.

the Johnsons recorded on the African plains to today's dwindling numbers. In Sabah (Borneo) the World Wildlife Fund requested photographs to assist in plans for a Martin and Osa Johnson Memorial Trail and Information Center along the Kinabatangan River. Their photographs hang on the walls of Walt Disney World's Animal Kingdom Lodge, a true testament to the lasting aura of their African work.

As cultural icons, Martin and Osa all but disappeared in the tense dialogues about racial stereotyping and environmental conservation throughout the 1960s, '70s, and '80s. During the last decade of the twentieth century, however, a renewed interest in their work reveals the ability of modern audiences to see beyond the discourses of the earlier part of the century. Osa's *I Married Adventure* was reissued in 1989 and again in 1997 (though unfortunately without its signature zebra-striped cover). A photograph of her astride one of Rattray's zebras has graced the cover of two separate books dedicated to female adventurers. Though she struggled to be recognized as an adventurer equal to her husband,

Osa has emerged in the twenty-first century as an extraordinary figure who stood with one foot in science and the other in popular culture. She negotiated a message of conservation for mainstream audiences that broached so-called elitist notions of the movement. By packaging conservation in tales of adventure, high fashion, and stuffed animals, Osa allowed consumers to quite literally buy into the idea that they were responsible for the fate of the world's wildlife.

BIBLIOGRAPHY

Akeley, Carl. *In Brightest Africa.* New York: Doubleday, 1923.

——. "Martin Johnson and His Expedition to Lake Paradise." *Natural History* 24 (1924): 284–88.

Akeley, Mary Jobe. *Carl Akeley's Africa: The Account of the Akeley-Eastman-Pomeroy Africa Hall Expedition.* New York: Dodd, Mead, and Co., 1929.

Ballard, Inez. "Do Women Make Good Explorers?" *The Sunday Eagle* (Wichita), September 25, 1932.

Bodry-Sanders, Penelope. *Carl Akeley: Africa's Collector, Africa's Savior.* New York: Paragon House, 1991.

Douglas, Robert Dick, Jr., David R. Martin Jr., and Douglas L. Oliver. *Three Boy Scouts in Africa: On Safari with Martin Johnson.* New York: G. P. Putnam's Sons, 1928.

Eastman, George. *Chronicles of an African Trip.* Rochester, NY: Private printing, 1927.

——. *Chronicles of a Second African Trip.* Edited by Kenneth M. Cameron. Rochester, NY: Friends of the University of Rochester Libraries, 1987.

——. "A Safari in Africa." With Audley D. Stewart. *Natural History* 27 (1927): 533–38.

Green, Fitzhugh. *Martin Johnson: Lion Hunter.* New York: G. P. Putnam's Sons, 1928.

Houston, Dick. "The Boy and Girl Next Door Made Movies Far Away." *Smithsonian* 17, 8 (1986): 144–55.

Hulme, Peter, and Russell McDougall, eds. *Writing, Travel, and Empire: In the Margins of Anthropology.* New York: I. B. Tauris, 2007.

Imperato, Pascal James, and Eleanor M. Imperato. *They Married Adventure: The Wandering Lives of Martin & Osa Johnson.* New Brunswick, NJ: Rutgers University Press, 1992.

Leigh, William R. *Frontiers of Enchantment: An Artist's Adventures in Africa*. New York: Simon and Schuster, 1940.

———. "Painting Backgrounds for the African Hall." *Natural History* 27 (1927): 575–82.

London, Charmian Kittredge. *The Book of Jack London*. New York: Century Company, 1921.

———. *Jack London and Hawaii*. London: Mills & Boon, 1918.

———. *The Log of the* Snark. New York: Macmillan Company, 1915.

———. *Our Hawaii*. New York: Macmillan Company, 1922.

London, Jack. *The Cruise of the* Snark. New York: Macmillan Company, 1919.

———. *Martin Eden*. New York: Macmillan Company, 1913.

———. *South Sea Tales*. New York: Macmillan Company, 1911.

Lundquist, James. *Jack London: Adventure, Ideas, and Fiction*. New York: Ungar, 1987.

Johnson, Martin. "Camera Safaris." *Natural History* 37 (1936): 46–62.

———. *Camera Trails in Africa*. New York and London: Putman's Sons, 1928.

———. *Cannibal-Land: Adventures with a Camera in the New Hebrides*. New York: Houghton Mifflin, 1922.

———. "Cannibals at the Movies." *Asia* 21 (1921): 568–611.

———. *Congorilla: Adventures with Pygmies and Gorillas in Africa*. New York: Brewer, Warren and Putnam, 1932.

———. "Into the African Blue." *Forest and Stream,* December 1929.

———. *Lion: African Adventure with the King of Beasts*. New York and London: Putnam's Sons, 1929.

———. "Long Shots from the Malekula Bush." *Asia* 21 (1921): 532–41.

———. *Over African Jungles: The Record of a Glorious Adventure over the Big Game Country of Africa 60,000 Miles by Airplane*. New York: Harcourt Brace, 1935.

———. *Safari: A Saga of the African Blue*. New York: Century Company, 1924.

——. "Sky Trails." *Natural History* 33 (1933): 131–38.

——. "Stalking Wild Animals with a Camera," *Asia* 23 (July 1923): 479–84, 537.

——. *Through the South Seas with Jack London*. New York: Dodd, Mead and Co., 1913.

——. "Wild Men of the New Hebrides." *Asia* 21 (1921): 568–611.

Johnson, Osa. "At Home in the Jungle." *Natural History* 27 (1927): 561–69.

——. *Bride in the Solomons*. Boston: Houghton Mifflin, 1944.

——. *Four Years in Paradise*. Mechanicsburg, PA: Stackpole Books, 2004.

——. *I Married Adventure*. New York: Kodansha Globe Books, 1997.

——. "Jungle." *American Magazine* 124 (1937): 146.

——. *Jungle Babies*. New York and London: Putnam's Sons, 1930.

——. "Jungle Dinner." *Hearst's International Cosmopolitan* 162 (1937): 74–79.

——. *Jungle Pets*. New York and London: Putman's Sons, 1932.

——. *Last Adventure: The Martin Johnsons in Borneo*. Edited by Pascal James Imperato. New York: William Morrow, 1966.

——. "My Home in the African Blue." *Good Housekeeping* 78 (1924): 48–49, 167–73.

——. *Osa Johnson's Jungle Friends*. Philadelphia and New York: Lippencott, 1939.

——. *Pantaloons: Adventures of a Baby Elephant*. New York: Random House, 1941.

——. *Snowball: Adventures of a Young Gorilla*. New York: Random House, 1942.

——. *Tarnish: The Story of a Lion Cub*. Chicago: Wilcox and Follett, 1944.

Kershaw, Alex. *Jack London: A Life*. New York: Macmillan, 1999.

Osborn, Henry Fairfield. "The Vanishing Wildlife of Africa." *Natural History* 27 (1927): 515–24.

Percival, A. Blayney. *A Game Ranger's Note Book.* New York: George H. Doran, 1924.

Preston, Douglas. *Dinosaurs in the Attic: An Excursion into the American Museum of Natural History.* New York: St. Martin's Press, 1986.

Quinn, Stephen Christopher. *Windows on Nature: The Great Habitat Dioramas of the American Museum of Natural History.* New York: Abrams, 2006.

Roosevelt, Theodore. *African Game Trails: An Account of the Wanderings of an American Hunter-Naturalist.* New York: Scribner's Sons, 1910.

Stange, Mary Zeiss. "Forward." In *Four Years in Paradise.* Mechanicsburg, PA: Stackpole Books, 2004.

Stasz, Clarice. *American Dreamers: Charmian and Jack London.* New York: St. Martin's Press, 1988.

Stott, Kenhelm W., Jr. *Exploring with Martin and Osa Johnson.* Chanute, KS: Martin and Osa Johnson Safari Museum Press, 1978.

Thomas, Lowell. "The Story of Martin Johnson." *Natural History* 39 (1937): 154–67.

Vaz, Mark Cotta. *Living Dangerously: The Adventures of Merian C. Cooper.* New York: Villard, 2005.

INDEX

Italicized page numbers indicate photographs.

Adventuring Johnsons (lecture film), 166
Africa. *See also* Africa, first expedition; Africa, second expedition
  climate, 74
  conservation, 92, 97–98, 132, 201, 203, 210
  economy, 76
  fifth expedition, 179–87, *181, 183, 186,* 190
  fourth expedition, 166–75, *171*
  gun laws, 81
  national parks of, first, 172
  South Seas compared to, 107
  third expedition, 160–66
Africa, first expedition
  films about, 130–33
  in Nairobi, 78–84, *83,* 104
  people and tribes of, 77–78, 91, 92, 95, 98–99, 102, 123
  safaris, 82, 83–86, 86–88, 88–94, 94–100, *99,* 100–104, 104–23, 135–37
  train to Nairobi, 74–78
Africa, second expedition
  challenges and changing environment, 147–48
  planning and funding, 131–32
  safaris, 135–46, *137, 139, 141,* 149–51, 151–54, 156–59
  traveling to, 134–35

airplane travel, 179–88, *181, 183, 186, 187,* 191–92, 196–97
Akeley, Carl
  African expeditions, 148–54
  cameras designed by, 138–39
  expedition and film support, 74, 131, 132–33
  grave of, 173
  illness and death, 153–54
  land preservation and national parks, 172
  letters to, 147
  lion research, 154, 162
  museum exhibitions named after, 173
Akeley, Mary, 149, 152
Akeley-Eastman-Pomeroy Expedition, 149–54, *151, 154*
Akeley Hall of African Mammals, 173
alcoholism, 167, 205
Alimbongo Mountains, 173
Aloni (servant), 79, 104, 115
Amala River, 100–104
American Museum of Natural History
  African exhibitions, 173, 176, 208
  children's education, *200*
  expedition sponsorship, 131–32
  film presentations at, 147
  films archived at, 130

orangutan exhibitions, 195
speciment-collecting
    expeditions for, 149–54, 185
Andrews, Roy Chapman, 165, 200
animal cruelty, 92, 203
Api, 60
Apia, 25
Archer's Post, 119–21
Athi River, 83–86, 86–88
Australia, 32, 47–48
automobiles, *83,* 83–84, 86–87,
    130, *137*
Ayers, Pat, 149

Baboona (film), 190
bathing taboos, 53
Belgian Congo, 161–62, 166–76,
    171, 188
Belonna Island, 31
Bessie (orangutan), 70, 72, 74
Big Game Hunt (television
    program), 205
Big Nambas tribe, 41–44, *43,* 49,
    50–54, *51*
blackbirding, 48, 50, 57
Boas, Franz, 5
Boculy (elephant tracker), 124–26,
    125, 136, *141,* 141–42, 145
Bora Bora, 22–24
Boran people, 109, 123, 145
Borneo, 62–72, *64, 67,* 191–96, *194,*
    195, 209
Borneo (film), 195–96
Boy Scouts, 165–66
Brower, Otto, 204
buffaloes, wild, 89, 90
Bujang (orangutan), 195
Bukhari (gorilla guide), 172–73,
    174, 175

buried alive rituals, 55
Burroughs, John, 24
Butler, Tom, 29–30

Campbell, William S., 174
cannibalism
    expedition with London, 27,
        28–30
    films about, 45–47
    first expedition, 37, 38–45
    second expedition, 47–54, 58,
        61, 61–62, 68
Cannibals of the South Seas
    (book), 46
Cannibals of the South Seas
    (film), 45–53
Carstens, Vern, 180, 181, 182,
    184, 188
Center Island, 184
Chaillu, Paul du, 174
Chapin, James P., 167
cheetahs, 144, 189, 201
children's charities, 201, 202
Chobe Hills, 113–19, 120
Chogoria Mission, 156, 158–59
clothing lines, 203
cobras, 70
Coca-Cola advertisements, 191
comic strips, 189
Congo (gorilla), 176
Congorilla (film), 176–78, *177*
conservation, 92, 97–98,
    132, 201, 203, 210
Cook, James, 13
Cooper, Merian, 161, 165, 174
Cotter, Bud, 101, 104
Crampton (commissioner), 108
Crane, John, 206–7
crocodiles, 65

Darbishire, George, 30
Darling, Ernest, 20, 22
Davis, Hugh, 181
Davison, Dot, 185
Davison, F. Trubee, 185, 199
Deelia (chief), 169–70
Doldrums, 15–16
Dorobo, 91, 92
Douglas, Dick, 166
Dryden, George, 167, 168–69, 201
Dryden, George Eastman, 167,
    168–69
Dugmore, A. Radclyffe, 80, 120

Eames, Roscoe, 4, 8, 9, 11
Eastman, George, 132–33, 134,
    149–54, 151, 160–62
Egypt, 167
elands, 97
elephants, 70–71, 95, 103, 126–29,
    128, 139, 141, 141, 144, 145–46, 191
Elmolos, 184
Embayo, 159
Embu, 106
Ernest (Frenchman), 22, 25
Espiritu Santo, 48, 61, 61–62
Europe, 3, 32, 159, 160–61, 167,
    188–89
Explorers Club, 73, 199–200

fashion, 159, 203
Fenelon, Gene, 11–12, 13, 14
Ferraragi (safari headman), 81, 84,
    91–92, 100, 104, 110
Fiji Islands, 26
films
    African animal, 130–33, 154–56,
        155, 160, 166–67, 168, 176–78,
        177, 190
    based on books, 205
    Borneo, 195–96, 199
    consulting for, 204
    with negative African
        imagery, 174
    popularity of African
        adventure, 156
    sound, 166–67, 168
    South Seas cannibals, 45–53
flesh-eating sores, 30, 31
Four Years in Paradise (Osa
    Johnson), 204
Froehlich, Conrad, 208
Fuji, 26

Getts, Clark, 196, 199, 204, 205,
    206, 208
gibbon apes. See Kalowatt
giraffes, 77, 96–97
Gore-Brown, Stewart, 182
gorillas, 172–75
Green, Fitzhugh, 166
Guadalcanal, 30–31
Guiana, 169

Hadji Mohammed Nur (chief),
    65, 66, 67
Haggard, Rider, 156
Harding, Thomas, 30
Hawaii, 9–15
headhouses, 54, 60
headhunters, 29, 68
heads, human, 54, 60, 61, 62
Helene (Tahitian girl), 21–22
Henry (sailor), 25, 31, 32
Hermann (Dutch sailor), 15, 16, 20
hippopotamuses, 118
Holmes (commissioner), 65,
    66, 70

homesickness, 47, 62, 134–35, 167–68
honey bears, 70
hyenas, 87, 122

I Married Adventure (film), 205
I Married Adventure (Osa Johnson), 83, 204–5, 209
Ingagi (film), 174
Isiolo River, 108–13 146–147
Ithanga Hills, 88–94
Ituri Forest, 162, 169, 188

Jansson, Arthur, 149
Japanda (safari skinner), 92
Jerramani (safari headman)
    disrespect, 100
    employment, 81
    gun laws and hunting, 84
    Lake Paradise safari, 104, 114, 115, 120, 122, 129
    lion sightings, 93
    masculinity issues, 89–90
    natives hunting pets, 91
Johnson, Freda, 4, 134
Johnson, John Alfred
    in Africa, 74–75, 80, 88, 89, 94, 104, 105, 121
    early years, 1–2, 33
Johnson, Lucinda (Constant), 1–2, 46
Johnson, Martin
    celebrity, 159, 166, 190–91
    childhood and family, 1–2
    death, 196–99
    early employment, 2–3, 33–34, 34, 36–37
    health, 30, 31, 157–59
    at Lake Paradise, 140

legacy, 208–9
marriage, 35–36
with Mbuti pygmies, *171*
with Osa, *83, 181, 209*
reviews about, 46
in Solomon Islands, *19, 40*
Johnson, Osa (Leighty)
    at American Museum of Natural History, *200*
    awards, 201, 203
    books by, 83, 166, 181, 204, 209
    celebrity, 45–46, 130, 159–60, 166, 190–91
    charity work, 201–2
    childhood and family, 34–35
    death, 206–7
    early employment, 35
    with Eastman, *151*
    with fish, *118*
    health, 37–38, 157–59, 167, 188, 189, 205–6
    at Lake Paradise, *139*
    at Lake Paradise with Boculy, *125, 141*
    lecture poster, *207*
    legacy, 206, 208–10
    with leopard and dog, *114*
    marriage to Getts, 204, 205
    marriage to Martin Johnson, 34, 35–36
    with Martin Johnson, *37, 83, 181, 209*
    with orangutan, *195*
    with Percival, *95*
    with pets, *67, 190*
Jungle Babies (Osa Johnson), 166, 181
Jungle Depths of Borneo (lecture film), 195, 199

Kaiser, Albert, 161–62
Kaisoot Desert, 121, 136, 149
Kalowatt (gibbon ape)
    adoption of, 66, *67*
    in America, 74, 133
    death of, 149
    first African expedition, 79, 88,
        90, 91, 104, 123
    traveling in South Seas with,
        70, 72
Kampia Tembo, 136
Kanakas, 23
Karo, 121
Kavairondo (camera carrier), 93
Kibondo, 173
Kikuyu, 104–5, 106
Kinabatangan River, *64,* 65–70,
    192–93, 209
King (commissioner), 60
King Kong (film), 174
King's African Rifles (KAR)
    army, 148
King Solomon's Mines (Haggard), 156
kissing, 188
Kiu, 77
Ku Klux Klan, 133

Lake Paradise (Mount Marsabit)
    from airplane, 183
    first expedition, 82, 113,
        125–29, *128*
    naming of, 126
    second expedition, 135–46, *137,*
        139, 140, 141, 149–51
Lake Rudolf (*now* Lake Turkana),
    183–84
Lamang, Borneo, 65
Laneri, Jim, 191, 192
Lazy Bones (mule), 144

lectures, 166, 176, 190, 195, 196,
    199, 201, *207*
Leigh, William, 149, 173
Leighty, Ruby Isabelle Holman
    "Belle," 34, 38, 208
Leighty, William Sherman,
    34, 189
leopards, 91–92, 94, 113, *114,* 187
Lion (Martin Johnson), 165, 166
lions
    Akeley and, 154, 162
    attacks on humans, 76
    behavior of, 109–12, 152–53,
        162–65, 185–86, *186*
    hunting, 93–94, 99, 100, 132,
        153, *154*
Livingstone, David, 204
London, Charmian, 4, *6,* 12, 29,
    30–31, 37–38
London, Jack, 3-4, *4, 5, 6, 7,* 37
London expedition, 3–31, *6, 10, 19*
Longania, 122
Lubenga Mission, 172
Lumbwa, 153, *154*

Maasai, 77–78, 95, 98–99, 102
Macdonough (veterinarian), 109,
    110, 112, 113
magazine articles, 130, 156, 166
Magollo (guide), 173
Malekula, 39–44, *43,* 48–60, *51*
Manua Islands, 24
Marjo (cheetah), 144
Marquesas Islands, 15, 16–18
Marsabit, 121, 122, 123–25
Martin, Dave, 166
Martin and Osa Johnson
    Memorial Trail and
    Information Center, 209

Martin Johnson: Lion Hunter
    (Green), 166
Martin Johnson Aerial
    Camera, 189
Martin Johnson Kodak Club, 180
Mazouyer, Paul, 50, 51, 54
Mbuti pygmies, 162, 169–72, *171,*
    188
Melville, Herman, 16, 17
Merille River, 121–22
Meru, 106–8
monkeys, 63–64, 68, 193–94
Moran, Charles, 56, 59, 60
Moreno, Robert, 181
Morway, Al, 181
Mount Kenya, 105–6, 156–59,
    186–87
Mount Kilimanjaro, 188
Mount Kinabalu, 192
Mount Marsabit, lake on. *See* Lake
    Paradise
Mount Mikeno, 154, 172, 173
'Mpishi (cook), 79–80, 104,
    115, 135
Murchison Falls, 162, 169
museums, 208. *See also* American
    Museum of Natural History

Nagapate (chief), 41, 42–44, *43,* 45,
    50–53, 54
Nairobi, 78–84, *83,* 104, 135, 153,
    162, 168, 182–83
Nakata (cabin boy), 15, 16, 23, 31
Nakuru (game-reserve
    patrolman), 95
nanti-dulu bush, 66
National Wildlife Federation,
    201, *202*
New Hebrides, 26–27, 48

Ngagi (gorilla), 176
Nile River, 161
Northey, Sir Edward, 80–81
Nowdi (chief), 56
Nuka Hiva, 16–19

Oliver, Douglas, 166
orangutans, 68–69, 70,
    194–95, *195*
Osafari, 203
Osa Johnson's Jungle Friends (Osa
    Johnson), 205
Osa's Ark (airplane), 181, 189, 191
Osborn, Henry Fairfield, 147
Osborn, Perry, 201

Pago Pago, 24–25
Pandassan, Borneo, 65
Pantaloons (Osa Johnson), 205
Parc National Albert, 172
Pawko (chief), 174–75
Pedler (East African Army
    officer), 109
Penangah, Borneo, 66–67
Percival, A. Blayney, 81–83, 86, 88,
    94–100, *95,* 129, 135, 137, 138
Percival, Phillip, 149, 152, 161
Perigo, Gail, 34
pets, 70, 144, 189, *190. See also*
    Kalowatt
pirates, 65
pneumonia, 157–59
Pomeroy, Daniel E., 131–32, 134,
    147, 149–54
Powler (captain), 60–61
Prin, Father, 39–41, 48
proboscis monkeys, 193–94
Putnam, George Palmer, 165
pygmies, 162, 169–72, *171,* 188

Quesada, Pete, 185

racism, 46
radio broadcasts, 159–60, 196
Raiatea, 22
Ramsaye, Terry, 130
Rattray, Andrew, 110–11, 112–13
recipes, 203–4
Red Summer, 46
Rennell Island, 31–32
rhinoceros, 96, 109, 116–19, 123–24, 142–43, 162
Rickenbacker, Eddie, 190
Ridgeway, Sir West, 63, 72
Ringgold Islands, 26
Roosevelt, Theodore, 24, 32, 81, 147

Safari (Martin Johnson), 165
safari, term translation and definition, 81
Sage, DeWitt, 167, 175
Salou (Mbuti pygmy), 169–70
Samoan Islands, 23–25
Sandakan, Borneo, 62–63, 192
Sanial, Arthur, 181
Serengeti Plains, 151–54, 162–65
Sergievsky, Boris, 181, 182
Simba (film), 154–56, *155*, 160
slavery, 48, 50, 57
Small Nambas tribe, 48–49
Smith, Arthur Donaldson, 82
snakes, 70, 102
Snark (boat), 4–32, *6*, 48
Snark Theater, 33–34, *34*, 35
Snowball (gorilla), 175–76
Snowball (Osa Johnson), 205
Society Islands, 20
Solomon Islands, 28–30, 38, *40*

Songa, *139*
Southern Game Reserve, 94–100, *99*
South Seas. *See also specific countries and islands*
    first expedition, 38–72, *40, 51, 61, 64, 67*
    with London, 3–31, *6, 10, 19*
    second expedition, 191–96, *194, 195*
spiders, 70
spirillum ticks, 120
Spirit of Africa [and Borneo] (airplane), 181, *181, 183,* 191
Spots (genet cat), 144
Stanley & Livingstone (film), 204
Stanton, Frank, 28
stealing, 60
Stevenson, Robert Louis, 16, 25
Stewart, Audley, 149
Stolz, Herbert "Bert," 4, 8
Sudan, Mohammed, 119
Sura, Bwana, 170

Tahaa, 22
Tahiti, 19–22
Tanganyika Territory, 152, 162, 168, *185,* 185–86
Tanna Island, 27–28
Tarzan films, 156
Taylor, Nancy Ann Wingfield, 35
Taylor, Stanley, 81
Tehei (navigator), 22, 23, 31
television programs, 205
Tenggara people, 67–68
Tethlong (chief), 49
Tilton, Joe, 191, 192, 199
toe deformities, 57, 58
Togichi, Paul H., 4, 6, 8, 12, 13

Toto Tembo (elephant), 191
toys, stuffed, 201, *202*
Trailing African Wild Animals
   (film), 130–33
Truson (orangutan), 194–95, *195*
Tsavo, 76
Turkanas, 184–85
Tutuila, 24–25
Typee (Melville), 17

Ugi, 30
Upolu, 25–26

Vao, 39, 48–50, 54–56, 60
vaudeville, 36–37
Virunga National Park, 172
Voi, 75–76
volcanoes, 25–26, 28

Wada (cook), 15, 23
Walsh, John, 86–88
water buffaloes, 64–65
water-vine stems, 66

Watt, Reverend, 27
Whitcomb, Frank, 26
Whitehead Plantation, 88–89
Wild Men of Africa (film), 156
Wiley (Polynesian trader), 27–28
Williams, Dick, 26
Wilsheusen, John, 156–59
Wings over Africa (lecture film), 190
With Stanley in Africa (film), 156
Wo-bang-an-ar (chief), 58
women of South Seas tribes,
   53, 55, 56
Wonders of the Congo (lecture
   film), 176

York, Duke and Duchess of,
   146–47

Zabenelli (butler), 79, 102, 104,
   105, 122
   zebras, *99*, 110–11
zoo donations, 176, 191, 195